The
Great
Reversal

Library of Congress Cataloging-in-Publication Data
Hinton, William.
 The great reversal : the privatization of China, 1978–1989 /
William Hinton.
  p.   cm.
 ISBN 0-85345-793-X : $28.00. — ISBN 0-85345-794-8 (pbk.) : $11.00
 1. Agriculture and state—China.   2. Communism and agriculture-
-China.   3. Collective farms—China.   4. Land reform—China.
 I. Title.
HD2098.H56   1989
338.1'851—dc20   89-13316
                                                        CIP

Monthly Review Press
122 West 27th Street
New York, N.Y. 10001

Manufactured in the United States of America

10 9 8 7 6 5 4 3 2 1

大回潮 Contents

Preface   7

Introduction: China's Rural Reforms   11

A Small Town in China: Long Bow 1978   31

A Trip to Fengyang County, 1983   48

Reform in Stride: Rural Change 1984   74

The Situation in the Grasslands, 1985   84

Reform Unravels: Rural Change 1986   95

Bypassed by Reform: Agricultural Mechanization 1986   110

Dazhai Revisited: 1987   124

Mao's Rural Policies Revisited   140

Why Not the Capitalist Road?   164

Tiananmen Massacre 1989   175

大回潮 Preface

June 4, 1989, stands as a stark watershed in China's modern history. The slaughter of unarmed civilians by units of the Peoples Liberation Army as they blasted their way to Tiananmen Square illuminated the "reform" era as nothing else could. It lit up, like a bolt of cosmic lightning, the reactionary essence of China's current leading group.

This essence was known to many in China and to some abroad long before the lightning struck in June 1989, but most members of the Western media and academic world were too mesmerized by China's reform rhetoric and market progress to apprehend the reality of the events unfolding before their eyes. Since privatization matched their prejudices and a consumption boom confirmed its validity, they preferred not to look too closely at the underlying currents of economic dislocation, infrastructural decay, environmental degradation, social disintegration, cultural malaise, and rising class antagonisms that threatened to unravel the fabric of Chinese society.

Mao Zedong was far more astute. More than twenty years ago during the Cultural Revolution, he exposed Deng Xiaoping, Yang Shangkun, and most of their "hard line" colleagues as capitalist roaders. He accurately predicted that if such persons ever came to power they would transform the Communist Party into a revisionist party and finally into a fascist party and then the whole of China would change color.

The surprising thing is not how accurate Mao's prediction turned out to be, but rather how quickly it materialized in history. The Third

Plenary Session of the Eleventh Central Committee, dominated by Deng, set out to "reform" China only eleven years ago. Big changes, such as family contracts for farmers and the exploitation of wage labor by private entrepreneurs, large and small, surfaced in a major way only five years ago. Yet in this short span unforeseen afflictions have so alienated the Chinese people, especially the urban dwellers most favored by reform, that in May and June 1989 they filled the streets with protesters from one end of China to the other.

Deng responded with guns and tanks that churned up the pavement of Changan Avenue, leaving thousands of dead and wounded in their wake. The moral bankruptcy of this ferocious military repression coupled with a revengeful nationwide hunt for culprits demonstrated to all who cared to see what the color of the reform really was and had been all along.

Make no mistake. The leaders in Beijing are not motivated by communist ideals; they are not revolutionary planners or socialist builders. They are newly constituted bureaucratic capitalists, busy carving the economy into gigantic family fiefs, ready, in true comprador style, to sell China out to the highest bidder. Their armed assault on the square was not an aberration but rather the culmination of a process that began when they first assumed leading posts after the death of Mao. They set out then to dismantle whatever socialist institutions, culture, customs, and habits the Chinese people had so painstakingly built up in the course of postliberation reconstruction. In doing so they put in motion a chain of events that led inexorably to confrontation with the whole Chinese people.

How, in so short a span of time, did Deng go from the status of admired hero, defiant yet irrepressible victim of the hated gang of four, to that of corrupt autocrat and bloodstained oppressor?

Part of the answer may be found in the reforms currently sweeping China. These essays chronicle and analyze the course of those reforms since the beginning, with the break-up of cooperative farming in the countryside. The collection makes a strong case for doubting the viability of any capitalist road strategy for China and asks whether China's reform leaders, having chosen just such a road, do not already show signs of degenerating into a group of bureaucratic capitalists similar to the Chiang Kaishek clique—the four-family junta that dominated China both politically and economically prior to liberation.

The events of June 3 and 4 point toward a conclusion that Deng and his colleagues have matured into just such a group. They used reform, particularly the openings provided by privatization and free-market trading, to parlay bureaucratic power into economic dominance at home, leading to comprador-type profit-sharing partnerships with multinationals abroad. This helps explain why, when faced with student demands for dialogue, for free speech, for truthful reporting, and for exposure of high cadres' personal assets Deng firmly rejected any and all concessions. At Tiananmen, it was not the future of the revolution that was at stake, it was the credibility of the dominant clique, its very mandate to rule. Any breach in the wall of secrecy surrounding wheeling and dealing by high cadres spelled "red alert" to Deng and his new emerging gang of four.

"It doesn't matter whether the cat is black or white, just so long as it can catch mice," Deng said in the early 1960s. This phrase, more than any other, made him famous. By the 1980s many people, observing the great man's social practice, came up with a phrase more apt: "It doesn't matter whether the cat is black or white, it doesn't even matter whether the cat can catch mice. What matters is that the cat not get caught."

With the students and the people of China hot on the track of the cat, the hunter became the hunted. Disdainful of consequences, he struck back.

大 Introduction:
回 China's
潮 Rural Reforms

The year 1988 marked the tenth year of what is known as the "reform" in China.* Since the reformers first applied their policies to the countryside the changes there have been thorough and far-reaching. Furthermore, they have been in place long enough to demonstrate not only an abundance of short-term consequences but also some long-term trends. At the start, the media in both China and the West could hardly praise rural reform enough, especially in regard to its results in crop production, but more recently a note of anxiety has crept into the news. Grain production, it seems, has stagnated. Both annual inputs and long-term investments have fallen. The agricultural infrastrucure has decayed and the environment, under fierce attack, has disintegrated. Internally, from top to bottom, an agonizing reappraisal has replaced self-congratulation.

How deep the questioning goes in China is anybody's guess. But from the frequency and urgency of the public appeals for patience, understanding, and steadfastness, the shock waves clearly run deep. Article after article begs the reader to understand that China is undergoing a great transformation, that good results are in the making but can never be achieved without hardship and sacrifice, that difficulties and reversals are inevitable and may last a long time. The authors of

---

*Since the usage of the word "reforms" to refer to these reactionary measures is widely accepted, I have conformed with this usage, and have henceforth avoided inserting quotation marks around the term. It should be clear from my analysis, however, that far from being reforms, the new policies amount to a counterrevolution.

11

these articles express few signs of contrition, few hints that there may be anything fundamentally wrong with the path that has been chosen. All the rising contradictions, all the accumulating costs are written off as "transitional," troubles that can and will be exorcized in time. They are not—to borrow a term from political scientist John Elster— "equilibrium features," built-in and inevitable negative consequences of the new policy, but merely transient ripples on the broad current of triumphant reform. Thus the call, as problems mount, is for more, deeper, faster change. Problems arise not from "too much, too fast," but from "too little, too slow." Worrisome inflation may require a pause, a mandatory period of consolidation, but that is only one small backward step in the grand march forward down the road to full privatization in the sphere of production and untrammeled freedom in the sphere of circulation. On the eve of the final decade of the twentieth century legions of Chinese economists, social scientists, and officials are eagerly rediscovering Adam Smith and busily engaged in reinventing the wheel—the great myth of the "free market." For them, all the profound and bitter lessons inflicted on China during the first nine decades of this century and the last six decades of the previous one seem to have faded quietly away into the mists of time, never to plague the living again. Foreign media pundits, almost without exception, echo these Chinese voices and urge them on toward new heights of pragmatism.

One might have expected a more sophisticated response both from within China and from without, but ever since Deng Xiaoping came to power and launched the reform in 1978 very few voices have been raised in criticism anywhere on the four seas or the six continents. In China many people, high and low, have indeed questioned and even protested, but although they have sparked continuous internal challenge and debate very little, if any, of the conflict has surfaced. Since all media are in the hands of those who support reform—whether the state, state-sponsored organizations, or private entrepreneurs, this is not surprising. But that hardly accounts for the lack of critical voices from abroad.

Meanwhile, in the United States, we seem to have arrived at a situation that curiously mirrors, in reverse image, the 1950s when I first returned after seven years participation in the Chinese Revolution.

Then I was one of a handful of persons speaking out in defense of what the Chinese people had wrought under Mao. Over the years the climate slowly changed. Here and there, concerned young scholars raised additional sympathetic voices. By 1972 even that diehard Nixon reversed himself, traveling to Beijing and beginning the legitimization of Mao's dominion in Western eyes. Thereafter China gained friends at an accelerating rate until by 1978, when Deng Xiaoping changed course, the whole Western establishment lined up in support. The experts quickly concluded, over Chinese protests, that the new course represented reform "capitalist style."

As Deng's policy unfolded to all but universal applause, I found myself sliding back into "glorious isolation" once more, a lonely if not entirely lone critic of what seemed to me to be an unnecessary and probably calamitous reversal of the self-reliant, planned national reconstruction of the previous thirty years.

I did not leap from defender to critic overnight, however. As an old friend of New China living abroad I was certainly free to speak out. But at the beginning of the reform period I consciously avoided passing hasty judgment. I decided, with uncharacteristic forbearance, to wait and see what the new regime, with most of the old heroes gone, would do. My particular concern was, of course, the countryside.

The reorganization of collective agriculture began in 1980 with a low-key Central Committee directive recommending the introduction of the "family contract system" on an experimental basis. Under this system, each family enters into a contract with the production brigade or village, which specifies its obligations to the state and the brigade. Anything the household produces beyond this it can keep. In remote areas, where the population was so scattered that meetings, work in common, and joint accounts made little sense, the family contract, or "responsibility system" was proposed as the "method where no other method would do." It never occurred to me that Deng would escalate this relatively noncontroversial, partial retreat from collective agriculture into the mass liquidation of the whole collective system in the countryside. In the course of time it became clear, however, that universal privatization was the goal and that the regime would pursue it with little regard for community preference, local conditions, or other special circumstances.

Noodle Land Triumphant

> After thirty years of uphill fight
> We're back to the old ways overnight.
> —Rhyme from the Northeast

Over the last ten years, a momentous decade of reform in China, I had a ringside seat at the edge, if not in the center, of the action. Every year but one after 1978 I spent from five to six months in China. For five years starting in 1980 I served as a consultant to the United Nations Grasslands Management Project in Wengniute Banner, Chao region, Inner Mongolia, some 600 miles northeast of Beijing. There we sought a solution to the problem of desertification. In the intervals between busy seasons at the project I also traveled, whenever possible, about an equal distance southwest to Long Bow village, Changzhi City, Shanxi province, where I helped the peasants launch an unprecedented experiment in comprehensive mechanization.

As the so-called reform challenged collective ownership throughout the countryside it soon came into conflict with both projects I was working on. Wengniute Ranch, as we called our huge spread of swamp, alkali flat, depleted range, and desert dune, was a unique, state-collective joint enterprise where a team of local herdsmen shared ownership, expressed as shares of stock, with the provincial government. This dual cooperative arrangement (a collective of herdsmen cooperating with the state) conflicted with the privatization drive of the reformers and the ambitions of some better off herdsmen who keenly wanted a chance to "get rich first." Together they fanned up local sentiment for liquidation.

After five years, after the investment of $4 million by the United Nations and an equal amount by the Chinese government, privatization brought the Grasslands Project to its knees. The regional government, refusing to consider any exception based on special circumstances, contracted all livestock, all hay lands, and most pastures back to individual herdsmen. In 1984, with the newly irrigated croplands also at risk and without cattle, sheep, or pastures with which to run grazing trails, the UN reluctantly withdrew, without having found the answers everyone sought to the problems posed by desertification. The machinery the UN brought remains at the site. Work goes forward in the form of custom services for individual contractors, but the project as conceived expired.

While this was happening on the northern frontier, down in the southeast corner of Shanxi province five years of heavy capital investment and hard work on the part of the peasants of Long Bow village also came to naught. In 1978, Long Bow villagers had begun the mechanization of almost 200 acres of corn with a collection of scrounged, tinkered, and homemade equipment that did everything from spreading manure to tilling land, planting seed, killing weeds, picking ears, drying kernels, and augering the kernels into storage. The twelve members of the machinery team multiplied labor productivity by a factor of fifteen while cutting the cost of raising grain almost in half. But when the reform, offering subsistence plots to all and contract parcels to the land hungry, broke the fields into myriad small pieces, comprehensive mechanization gave way perforce to intermittent plowing and planting. This left the peasants no alternative but to abandon most of their advanced equipment and reactivate their hoes. When the bank asked for its loan money back the village head said "take the machinery." But the bank never found a buyer, so to this day the manure spreaders, the smoothing harrows, the sprayers, the sprinkle irrigation sets, the corn pickers, and the grain dryers lie rusting in the machinery yard, mute testimony to a bygone—or is it a bypassed?—era.

These two experiences shook me. Not only had I personally put a lot of effort, sweat, and pain into both projects, I knew how much others had also contributed, how much store they set on success and how important that success was to China's future. But the circumstances, in both cases, were exceptional. State-collective joint enterprises were rare indeed, even more rare, it seems, than mechanized villages. One could hardly fault the whole reform because of two stillborn experiments, though one certainly could fault the mindless, dogmatic way the local functionaries applied it.

At about that time an experience of a different sort brought home to me how far beyond the remote mountain hamlets mentioned in the original Central Committee directive the so-called reform had spread. In the summer of 1983 I flew by plane from Beijing to Shanghai. From my comfortable seat 30,000 feet up I saw for the first time the vast extent and astonishing physical results of the "responsibility system" on the North China plain.

I looked down in growing disbelief and I wept. Where once, under a seamless web of adobe villages and their linking roads, clear squares and oblongs of land—green, yellow, and brown—had stretched unbroken to the horizon, now 1,000 kilometers of miniscule strips crowding first in one direction, then in another, in haphazard, never duplicated patterns. This was not "postage stamp" land such as used to exist before land reform, but "ribbon land," "spaghetti land," "noodle land"—strips so narrow that often not even the right wheel of a cart could travel down one man's land without the left wheel pressing down on the land of another.

After decades of revolutionary struggle, after China's peasants had finally managed to create a scale and an institutional form for agriculture that held out some promise for the future, some promise that the tillers could at last lay down their hoes and enter the modern world more-or-less in step with their hi-tech-oriented, machine-savvy urban fellow citizens—it had come to this! With one blip on the screen of time, scale and institution both dissolved. The latest page in the great book of history barely rustled as it turned hundreds of millions back to square one.

A stunned peasant comrade said to me, "With this reform the Communist Party has shrugged off the burden of the peasantry. From now on, fuck your mother, if you get left behind blame yourself."

I was aware that many millions of peasants welcomed reform, that many villages had stagnated as cooperatives, and that the privatization of use rights to the land coupled with sharp price increases for farm produce and the right to engage at will in whatever sidelines caught one's fancy had brought many independent operators a welcome measure of prosperity.

Nevertheless, to me, the irrational fragmentation alone meant the eventual neutralization of whatever advantages the government saw in it or had served up with it to make it palatable. "Noodle land" could only lead, in the long run, to a dead end. I could not think of any place in the world where rural smallholders were faring well, certainly not smallholders with only a fraction of a hectare to their names and that in scattered fragments. The low output of peasants farming with hoes meant that on the average each full-time laborer could produce about a ton of grain a year, one eight-hundredth of the amount I harvested farming with tractors in Pennsylvania. And that ton of grain, worth about $100, would determine the standard of living for countless tillers of the land far into the future. Whatever prosperity any peasant now enjoyed was bound to be ephemeral as the gap between industry and agriculture, city and country, mental and manual labor expanded and the relentless price scissors imposed by the free market opened wide.

One Step Forward, Two Steps Back

> Think it, say it, do it, screw it.
> Everything ends in a mess!
> —Rhyme on pragmatism from rural Shanxi

Some of the early results of the "responsibility system," however, seemed to prove my fears wrong. The income of many "noodle land" contractors increased beyond most expectations. Behind this rise lay not only the big price increases decreed for many farm products but also the bonuses paid by the state for above-quota deliveries. Peasants in previously stagnant villages found these bonuses easier to earn now that ample supplies of fertilizers and pesticides, long in the pipeline, found their way onto the market. At the same time many individuals who chose not to contract land for commodity grain or lost out in the scramble for contracts, went out to seek their fortunes elsewhere and by other means. Less than half of them found work at first, but among those that did—artisans, peddlers, carters, construction workers, and day laborers of all sorts—there were many whose income also increased. And so, as the reform gathered momentum, prosperity came to many in the countryside. Contrary to my expectations, yields generally held their own or even went up at first, at least on the charts (government statisticians never hesitated to make the most of what, viewed soberly, were no more than crop estimates), and on top of that the output of commercial crops—cotton, oil seeds, tobacco, and other specialty products—suddenly favored with incentive prices, rose even faster. Add the receipts from these sources at enhanced prices to the receipts from off-the-farm labor at enhanced wages, and one has the basis for a lively expansion of the rural economy.

In 1984, the government reported and celebrated an historic breakthrough in grain production—a gross harvest of over 400 million long tons. So much commodity grain appeared for sale that the price of free market grain fell to almost the same level as that of state-controlled grain. This generated euphoria in regard to reform. Responsible officials decided that the grain problem had been solved and trade negotiators began to discuss contracts for substantial exports of feed grains. The reform, it seemed, was really working, at least on the production front. If there were serious questions they were about where the privatized new society was heading. Did the reform road lead to socialism?

With prosperity breaking out all over (progress actually was very uneven), not too many people seemed to care about end results. Nevertheless, given the Communist Party's long-standing commitment to socialism and mindful of Mao's dictum that the only road open to China was the socialist road, the "reformers" wooed the "diehards" (or was it the waverers?) with polemics that reconfirmed socialism as the goal while fundamentally redefining what the word meant. Certain theoreticians turned to this task with a will. Since at that point they had not yet discovered the "first stage of socialism," an umbrella stage that could justify just about any economic behavior, they reduced socialism to (1) public ownership (the land still belongs to the state), and (2) payment according to work (each contracting peasant family takes responsibility for its own profits and losses).

When no one could deny any longer that many peasants (fish pond operators, orchard magnates, and laying hen tycoons—the new darlings of the press) were hiring their neighbors and pocketing big profits, the theorists declared managing to be legitimate work (which was never in dispute), but failed to make any distinction between return on capital invested and payment for services rendered. They lumped both these things together as the legitimate rewards of entrepreneurial effort. Thus surplus value disappeared and along with it exploitation. "How can there be exploitation," they asked, "when the employees earn more at their new jobs than they did as peasants?"

This "fair day's pay for a fair day's work" logic laid exploitation fears to rest, at least for the uninitiated. The Central Committee decided that hiring wage labor was all right, even desirable, so long as the number of workers did not exceed eight. Establishments with up to eight workers it called "individual enterprises." It considered workers in these enterprises, most of whom were indeed often relatives, to be family members. If there was any surplus value it remained in the family, so to speak. But soon knottier problems arose, in the form of newly rich entrepreneurs who built and owned whole factories and employed hundreds, even thousands, of workers. They really did look like, talk like, earn like, and spend like capitalists. No one could maintain that their workers were all family, nor could anyone maintain that the wages they paid or the conditions they granted were fair. Since theory could not exorcize such "devils" it soon made room for them with a proposition as eclectic as the still to be invented "first stage of socialism." The new apologia went more or less like this: socialism, as everyone knows, requires an advanced level of productive forces; therefore, whatever stimulates production *ipso facto* advances the cause of socialism. Economic development, by definition, turns into socialist progress. Deng always put the emphasis on "catching mice," by which he meant producing goods and services by any method that worked, including that good old-fashioned method, private investment for private profit—what my old colleague, Archie Wright, the leader of the New York State Dairy Farmer's Union, used to call "making a dollar like a dollar ought-a-be made." Based on this type of reasoning, the Central Committee then created a new category of enterprise called "private," a category that had no limits.

When translated into social reality this pragmatism quickly produced all sorts of anomalies, contradictions, and conflicts, foremost among which was accelerated social polarization throughout a society, both urban and rural, where classes and class struggle had been declared passé. By polarization I mean class differentiation, primarily the large-scale shift from peasant smallholder (in cooperative China this meant community shareholder) to wage laborer, and at the same time, the small-scale counter shift from peasant smallholder to capitalist (mostly petty). The vast majority, it goes without saying, took part in the former transformation, dropping out of their birthright, petty bourgeois class status, and landing in the working class, probably the most massive class transfer in world history. And it took place without mechanization of crop production by drawing off some of the surplus population backed up on the land. Taking part in the transfer were some who did not want to contract land and many who were unable to do so due to age, health, gender, lack of labor power, or lack of the means to farm.

The transfer of millions into the working class had a unique aspect, however. In the majority of cases the individuals involved and their families still retained a share of per capita grain land, a subsistence plot or plots that could provide food for survival but not enough income to live on. In so far as their main source of livelihood was concerned, these men and women became wage workers, but they did not forego all land-use rights. They simply abstained or lost out in the scramble for contract rights to land used for commodity production. Some of the implications of this for China's future development are discussed in the final essay, "Why Not the Capitalist Road?"

Next to social polarization, the most striking consequence of reform was the far-reaching cultural regression. Privatization, by returning the rural economy to something closely resembling pre-revolutionary China (even to the generation of large contractors who subcontracted the extended land-use rights they usurped just as subletting landlords of old had done) brought with it, a revival of all the worst features of the old society—prostitution, gambling, drug abuse, and the proliferation of underworld gangs that controlled and profited from these phenomena. In the cultural sphere, old customs, old habits, old ideology, and old superstitions, all bearing a distinctly feudal flavor, also surfaced. On their own once more, without the collective strength to tackle the challenges of the environment, families tended to fall back on the cultural props of the past, such as shrines to the earth god, the kitchen god, the fertility god, and others. The newest building in Long Bow village is a temple to the earth god. They also revived in ever more blatant form all the traditional ceremonies that mark progress through life from birth to death, paying more exorbitant brideprices, arranging more lavish weddings and more extravagant funerals, building more elaborate tombs and borrowing more money at more usurious rates to pay for all these excesses. Commitment to scientific rationalism receded along with all the emphasis on simplicity, frugality, and thrift that the revolution had tried so hard, without success, to propagate and consolidate.

Cultural regression inside the Communist Party rivaled the regression in society as a whole. Once the party told the peasants to enrich themselves, communists had, perforce, to lead the way. Otherwise nobody would believe that the party meant to stand by those who made out well at production or in the marketplace. The scramble for personal advantage undermined whatever standards of communist conduct remained. Corruption, as abuse of privilege, had long been a serious problem linked to power holding in the collective system. Transformed now by the growing cash nexus, corruption as profit taking spread far and wide, from low to high and from high to low. Graft, kickbacks, and illegal speculation multiplied, sinking the party's prestige, what was left of it, to new lows. Most alarming, the country could no longer count on cadres, high or low, to put national interest first when dealing with foreign nationals and, more to the point, multinationals. At this level cultural regression threatened China's hard-won autonomy, the fruit of more than one hundred years of bitter struggle.

Finally the reform unleashed in its wake an unprecedented attack on the environment. By making each family responsible for its own profit and loss the new policy changed the goal of economic effort from the long-term maximization of yields and other outputs through the mobilization of all skills, talents, and resources to the short-term maximization of family income. This change sent hundreds of millions out looking for anything that might turn an instant profit or be converted to immediate benefit. Thus began a wholesale attack on an already much-abused and enervated environment, on mountain slopes, on trees, on water resources, on grasslands, on fishing grounds, on wildlife, on minerals underground, on anything that could be cut down, plowed up, pumped over, dug out, shot dead, or carried away. During the collective period the state had reserved such things as mineral and timber rights to itself, but allowed some local exploitation under controlled conditions (unfortunately often violated). The state had also regulated (not always successfully) the use of steep mountain slopes, grasslands, large bodies of water, and other fragile ecosystems. Many peasant communities, for mutual benefit, also established and enforced some controls on the exploitation of local resources. With the reform, communities lost their clout in such matters and the state not only relaxed its regulations, but could no longer enforce those that still stood.

I concluded from the experiences of those years that what the Deng group was building in China was not socialism, but something much closer to the old mixed economy of the New Democracy period which the revolution brought into being in the early 1950s with the successful completion of land reform—a combination of public, private, joint public-private, and cooperatively owned enterprises. While it seemed that this was working reasonably well, it also seemed that from a socialist perspective it was very unstable. The most dynamic sector of industry, transport, and trade was the private sector. While it was still small in percentage terms it boasted the most rapid rate of growth. By contracting large chunks of publicly owned industry to individual managers the government was in effect privatizing the public sector as well. When one added to this the already completed, all but universal privatization of agriculture it became clear that: (1) the vast majority of Chinese, the peasants, were already functioning in a free enterprise environment; (2) the nonfarm private sector would soon be substantial; and (3) the public sector of the economy allocated by contract and concession to individual managers was headed in the same direction. This did not seem to be a very solid formula for building socialism.

Beginning in autumn 1985, the euphoria concerning the progress brought about by reform in China began to wane. The 1985 crop report issued by the Ministry of Agriculture showed a shocking drop of 30 million tons. Alternative figures from competing ministries showed a shortfall closer to 50 million tons. Everyone finally agreed on 25 million, though where that figure came from is obscure. Since the weather had not been particularly bad there seemed to be no rational explanation for the setback. Some authorities blamed it on price fluctuations, on price promises broken by state grain stations when confronted with the 1984 glut.

It seems clear now that the problem lay not with the 1985 crop but with the figures on the 1984 crop. The harvest of 1984 was never a record breaker. It was only normal or near normal. Most of the great increase registered that fall came out of collective storage. It found its way onto the market after the collectives broke up and dispersed their assets to their members. The sudden flow of grain all but broke the market because the government, fearing possible shortfalls with the family contract system, had simultaneously brought in millions of tons of grain from overseas. "We were all eating Canadian wheat that winter," said a Beijing resident.

Since China's peasants had not in fact produced 405 million tons in

1984 they could not subsequently duplicate the record "harvest" of that year. The reformers' most celebrated success turned out to be a phantom. The specter of chronic grain shortages sobered the whole country. In retrospect, the year 1985 proved to be a turning point in other fields as well, for that was the year when speculators in high positions, taking advantage of the new dual price system, raised official corruption not only to new quantitative but also to new qualitative levels. At the same time decentralization, some devolution of central power downward, allowed provinces and even some municipalities to act as virtual independent kingdoms in the realm of trade. On the one hand they set up barriers to interprovincial trade when it was advantageous to them— hoarding scarce resources or commodities, for instance—on the other they entered into huge foreign trade deals that brought in a flood of hard consumer items, including automobiles, at exorbitant prices. Thus they quickly ran through a large part of the nation's foreign currency reserves. China ran up an adverse trade balance of $15 billion that year, the bulk of it with Japan, and the imports undercut some struggling native industries.

During the same period capital investment soared, but far too little of it went into productive enterprises and far too much into nonproductive projects such as housing (mainly urban high-rise apartments), office buildings, recreation facilities, and underbooked luxury hotels. Every division of the government tried to get in on the huge profits anticipated from the foreign tourist trade, but only a few succeeded. At the same time no unit could launch major projects to improve the agricultural infrastructure because without the cooperative system nobody could mobilize peasants for work without paying cash wages, and no unit had that kind of cash.

All the spending without compensating production brought on inflation, particularly the inflation of food prices which hit urban residents hard. They were already spending half their incomes on food. But inflation hit industrial commodities as well, particularly the fuel, fertilizer, pesticides, and machinery needed by peasants to grow crops, which forced them to buy less and adversely affected yields.

Thus 1985 was the year when the chickens began to come home to roost, when the impetus that the reform gave to the economy began to unravel. All the contradictions generated by direct and contracted privatization combined with the half steps taken to transfer decision-making from government offices to the marketplace sharpened. By the time October came around masses of students were marching in the streets of major cities throughout the country protesting the flood of Japanese goods, rising prices, and spreading corruption.

Since then, the dislocations inside China have continued to escalate. While the reassertion of stricter controls from the center has reduced the trade imbalance somewhat, nonproductive capital expenditures are still out of hand. The inflation rate is higher than ever, leading in late 1988 to an epidemic of runs on banks. All other problems, crime, birth rates, population growth, epidemic diseases, environmental destruction and, last but not least, shortfalls in grain production are getting worse. In 1988, blaming bad weather, the government reported a drop of over 9 million tons in grain production and this was probably an understatement. Some city dwellers now have to take coarse grains along with the fine in their grain ration. Peasants are killing off chickens, pigs, and even slaughtering dairy cows because there are not enough coarse grains to go around.

The question raised by all these developments is no longer: Does this road lead to socialism or capitalism? The capitalist character of the road is pretty clear. The question is: Does the road lead forward or backward?

Reviling Models

> In the 1950s we helped one another.
> In the 1960s we denounced one another.
> In the 1970s we doubted one another.
> In the 1980s we swindled one another.
> —Rhyme from rural Shanxi

It is against the background of China's rapidly unfolding transformation, beginning late in 1978, filtered through my own slowly maturing perception and understanding, that over a period of ten years I put together the essays in this book.

I have chosen to begin with my story of Long Bow village. This appeared in 1979, a few months after the Central Committee of the Chinese Communist Party met in plenary session to launch the great policy reversal. It is important to the whole thrust of this volume because it describes a thriving cooperative village which at the time was following Mao's formula for success—"Take grain as the key link, pay attention to animal husbandry, forestry, fish raising, and sideline occupations, and develop an all-around rural economy." To this five-point charter Long Bow had added a successful program of agricultural mechanization.

Long Bow's story, prior to the introduction of reforms there in December 1982, illustrates what peasants could do by working together, pooling brains, brawn, and resources to create an advanced community. On their own they would never have divided their fields or contracted out their industries. They yielded to orders from above. Since then, the community has prospered with the rapid industrial and commercial growth of the whole district, but while much has gone well, much has also gone wrong, particularly on the land. It would be hard to argue that this community is better off today, seven years later, than it would have been had it remained a cooperative.

"A Trip to Fengyang County" was written after a 1983 visit to Anhui province at the invitation of Vice-Premier Wan Li. There I saw the best the reform had to offer in rural development, but I also saw a host of problems arising from the privatization and atomization of the land, the most serious being the polarization of society, the emergence of affluent entrepreneurs and shareholders on the one hand and of wage laborers on the other.

Thereafter, with each passing season, negative trends grew and multiplied in the countryside and society at large. I tried to sum up the new situation in two pieces, one initially a lecture, and one a long letter, which are here presented as "Reform in Stride" and "Reform Unravels." While the first raised the question of whether the road taken could lead to socialism, the second raised doubts about the reformers' ability to promote sustained, stable growth under any label, and particularly about their ability to create a prosperous, independent, autonomous China in a world dominated by the United States, European, and Japanese capital.

The other two articles from the middle 1980s, "The Situation in the Grasslands" and "Agricultural Mechanization," deal with technical problems of internal development. They do not directly challenge reform policy, but they do disclose some of the critical roadblocks these policies have placed in the way of range preservation and farm mechanization.

"Dazhai Revisited" was written in the fall of 1987 in response to several news stories in the Chinese press which revived attacks on the past history of the peasant community Mao chose as a model and went on to exaggerate and embellish the community's progress since it ceased functioning as a collective in 1983. I concluded that the Chinese media had consistently misrepresented Dazhai, disparaging collective achievements on the one hand and idolizing reform achievements on the other, with equal disregard for facts in both cases. The most salient fact was that in 1987, according to official figures, Dazhai peasants did not raise enough grain to feed themselves.

The attack on Dazhai was in reality an attack on Mao. Since learning from Dazhai as a model in agriculture was one of the focal points of Mao's rural policy, the denunciation was part of the rejection of that policy. This conclusion, supported by a correspondence piece by Herb and Ruth Gamberg in *Monthly Review* in September 1988, stirred Hugh Deane, former World War II correspondent in China and a leader of the U.S.-China Friendship Association, to respond. While agreeing with our position that Dazhai had been falsely denigrated, he asserted that Dazhai's achievements notwithstanding, rural failures outweighed the rural successes achieved by Mao and some of the failures amounted to catastrophes. He called the famine that followed the Great Leap the "worst in human history" and went on to compile an indictment of Mao that can stand as a fairly comprehensive and exemplary elaboration of the reform group's objection to the man, his policies, and his deeds. "Mao's Rural Policies Revisited" was written originally in defense of Mao and in rebuttal to this one-sided evaluation of his role in the postliberation history of China. The article entitled "Why Not the Capitalist Road?" is an attempt to summarize and bring up to date Mao's thesis that the capitalist road was not and is not open to China in the twentieth century.

Patterns Shrewd and Dire

> Ten hundred million alive in our fair nation.
> Nine hundred million deep in speculation.
> One hundred million primed to join the operation.
> —Beijing rhyme, 1989

Looking back on the ten years covered here one can see certain patterns that were not very obvious when the decade began. One of these pertains to the method followed by the reformers. Throughout the whole course of the reform the method has been the same—to take a small, more or less minor, and therefore not highly controversial, aspect of the socialist base or superstructure as the target for "experimentation," and then escalate the experiment into a total transformation not only of the original target but of the whole class of phenomena it represents, on the grounds that the "experiment" worked. Pursuing this piecemeal, indirect approach the reformers avoid confrontation with those formidable social forces in society that might congeal to defend the collective system if the attack came head on. By the time any would-be defenders wake up to what is actually happening they are faced with a *fait accompli:* the whole institution or practice under attack has already undergone radical transformation.

Deng first used piecemeal methods to privatize agriculture, then applied them to the legitimization of the private exploitation of wage labor. A policy that had originally frowned on any and all private hiring was belatedly amended to approve "individual" enterprises that hired no more than eight workers, then relaxed to approve "private" enterprises that employed hundreds, even thousands, of workers. It took only a year or two to go from no exploitation to "anything goes." State leaders justified the "private" category as essential to the recently discovered "primary stage" of socialism. The goal by the end of 1988, it seemed, was to have private individuals own 30 percent of the industrial plant outright, while professional managers contracted to run the residual state-owned sector unit by unit. Meanwhile, the state planned to sell off its equity in the industrial sphere in the form of stock to plant workers, individually managed state units, and private entrepreneurs.

The reformers repeated this type of metaphoric sleight of hand over and over again to the point where it became clear that the reform had never been an openminded, trial-and-error search for an alternative "Chinese road to socialism." The leaders were not "feeling out the stepping stones in order to cross the river"—as Deng maintained—but rather conducting a disguised frontal attack on the whole socialist system, designed in advance to replace it with production relations, an ownership system, institutions, customs, and culture compatible with private enterprise and free market exchange.

The second pattern that one sees emerging over the years creates a sense of déjà vu. What the Chinese people are confronting with the accelerating growth of privilege and corruption at the top while inflation undermines the living standards of ever-wider circles of citizenry at the bottom, looks like a reply of sad scenes from a bygone era, the late 1920s and early 1930s: the disintegration of the nationalist revolution launched by Sun Yatsen, and the degeneration of a revolutionary party that came earlier to power, the Guomindang.

Communists suppressed corruption after their victory in 1949, but never completely conquered it. With the reform, new forms have arisen. A qualitative leap occurred when, in 1985, the reformers created the dual price system. They applied it as a step toward replacing the much-disparaged planned economy with the assumed impartial regulation of the marketplace by the "invisible hand" of competition. But dual pricing opened the way for a vast escalation of corruption in the form of bureaucratic profiteering that observers quickly dubbed the "official turnaround." The term, as described by the dissident astrophysicist Fang Lizhi, refers to the "use of official power and connections to procure commodities or other resources at low prices in the state-run sector of the economy, then turning around to sell them at huge mark-ups within the private sector.[1] Proliferating official turnaround virtually annulled any benefit that the dual price system might have provided and greatly aggravated the inflation that had already reached alarming levels.

The enrichment of high cadres by means of such speculation is now combined with the mass entry of high cadres' children into every kind of corporate activity, especially the lucrative import and export business (the law forbids officeholders themselves from engaging in busi-

---

1. Fang Lizhi, "China's Despair and China's Hope," *New York Review of Books*, February 2, 1989, pp. 3–4.

ness). Together the two trends threaten to recreate something similar to the bureaucratic capital that dominated China prior to 1949.

Astute observers, among them the dissident journalist Liu Binyan, have already issued warnings. "A large number of Chinese worry," Liu writes, "that on the mainland there will appear again a group that uses its official position to become a comprador class, the likes of Chiang Kaishek, T.V. Soong, Kong Xiungxi, and the Chen brothers Chen Guofu and Chen Lifu. This kind of worry is not without reason."[2] Now that China has opened wide, virtually removing the proverbial door from its hinges, could the final result of the interaction between world finance and corrupt bureaucracy be, as Liu Binyan projects, not a national but a new comprador bourgeoisie with all the threats to independence and autonomous development that that implies?" Taking the capitalist road, it seems, has consequences which no one can either justify or control.

After Tiananmen

> Once the party, like the sun
> Lit up the land with steadfast rays.
> Now the party, like the moon
> Changes every fifteen days.
> —Rhyme from southeast Shanxi

The last article in this volume is based on a public lecture on the prodemocracy movement in China. It emphasizes above all the mass participation of the citizens of Beijing in blocking the army from entering that city to disperse the students. Such overwhelming mass participation, rare in history, was duplicated in various forms all across China, both before and after the massacre, and reflected jarring dissatisfaction with the state of the nation and the direction of economic and social drift after the reform took hold.

Both the extraordinary breadth of the nationwide protest and the ruthless killing used to suppress it revealed the extent of the crisis Deng's pragmatism had brought on China. The people could not accept

---

2. Liu Binyang, "The Relationship Between Politics and Economics," The Alexander Epstein Memorial Lecture, University of Michigan, October 20, 1988, p. 5.

the consequences of the privatization wind Deng blew up, and he and his clique could not accept the consequences of any democratic concessions, token or otherwise, that might limit their power to run China as they pleased. The result was a tense, confrontational standoff between a disaffected population and a handful of autocrats stripped of any credible mandate to rule. Large numbers of Communist Party members, government functionaries, and army personnel now side with the people in demanding change. But no one, certainly not any of the students who sparked the protest, has come forward with a coherent explanation of what went wrong or a viable policy for putting things right. Appalled by the living results of the capitalist road, most people nevertheless fail to see the causal links between these results and the policies, the political line, that brought them about.

However, the lurid light cast on the regime and its works by the massacre on the road to Tiananmen is forcing everyone to analyze and reappraise the experience of the last decade. Calling for democracy, freedom, and more reform can hardly suffice as a response to wholesale killing and repression by self-styled reformers. People must confront and expose the pseudosocialist rhetoric that now, more than ever, masks the capitalist road, make some clear choices in favor of renewed, self-reliant socialist transformation, and prepare for protracted struggle.

大回潮 A Small Town in China: Long Bow 1978

Thirty years ago, the sounds heard in the village of Long Bow were country sounds—cocks crowing in the darkness before dawn, giant millstones creaking as they were pushed around their rough stone beds by hand, the hoarse bellow of the village chairman announcing a meeting through a megaphone from the tower of the expropriated Catholic church. The loudest sound then, and one that still haunts memory, was the crashing of the massive wooden wheel hubs against the beams of the heavily laden carts as they traveled along the frozen ruts of the roads in winter. From a distance it sounded like some tireless netherworld kettledrummer.

Today, the dominant sound in Long Bow is no longer a country sound but the shrill wail of steam locomotives in the railroad shops, testing their eerie voices against a background roar of army tanks racing across the proving grounds on the flanks of Great Ridge Hill. There is an accompanying cacophany of truck, bus, and jeep horns on the highway as frustrated drivers try to make their way through a stream of hand-carts, donkey carts, tractor-drawn wagons, bicycles, and pedestrians.

Inside the village, a lesser background roar rolls from the big grinder of the production brigade's cement plant, while from the long shed that was once a meeting hall, the high whine of carborundum on steel shreds the air. There, young women working in shifts around the clock polish saw blades that will be exported to Tanzania.

This article originally appeared in *Geo* magazine, June 1980, and is reprinted by permission.

The tower of the old church was torn down long ago. The brigade leaders have installed a loudspeaker on the roof of their headquarters, and their booming voices can be heard in the farthest fields. For many years, they relied on loudspeaker "broadcasts" to regulate the collective production that came into full flower in 1958. The loudspeaker blasted forth before dawn to wake people up, at noon to summon them from the fields, and at sundown to signal that the day's work was done. But the music that rang out over the years was not "The East Is Red," that solemn hymn to Mao Zedong that dominated China; it was a lively Shanxi folk tune rendered on a double-reed horn (a cross between an oboe and a trumpet) and several Chinese snakeskin fiddles. Inside the village, the amplified jam session made eardrums ache. Out on the garden land of the First Production Team, half a mile away, it sounded like a wedding dance for elves, leprechauns, wood sprites, and fox spirits.

In 1979, individual earnings were brought more closely in line with individual effort, so that material reward became the primary incentive to hard work. At the same time electronic exhortation, discipline by loudspeaker, was abandoned. The air over the village was turned back to the cocks that still crow before dawn and the peddlers who still hawk their wares in the alleys. But they can never hope to recapture the attention they once took for granted. There is too much background noise from the many locomotives in the railroad yards.

As things used to be, one could look down from the summit of Great Ridge Hill and see the whole of Long Bow stretched out on the plain like a map. The polarization of village society was clearly revealed by the contrast between the adobe huts of the poor peasants and hired laborers, roofed with mud and straw, and the high brick dwellings of the landlords and rich peasants, roofed with tile. Gentry families occupied whole courtyards while poor peasants bedded down in whatever ramshackle sections of walled enclosure they could find. That was before the land reform giving land to individual peasants, which took place in Shanxi in 1945 and reached South China in 1950.

Today, all that can be seen from the hill is a mass of greenery. A special crew began to plant trees in Long Bow as soon as the cooperative was created by the land-pooling movement in 1954. In the intervening years, more than 250,000 trees have been planted, and they have transformed the whole character of the settlement. The desolate, sunbaked, semiruined earthworks of the past, open to all the violence of heaven, have become a cool, shaded, gardenlike complex of interlocking courtyards, streets, and alleys that offer protection against the extremes of all seasons.

Beneath the green of the newly planted trees, the predominant color of most Chinese villages in the North is still the glowing tan of natural adobe. Not so Long Bow. When the brigade leaders heard that foreign guests were coming in 1971, they mobilized the whole community to whitewash the walls on both sides of all the main streets, making the predominant color a dazzling white. The ever present crimson slogans stand out on this background as if molded in three dimensions. Whitewashing apparently pleased the inhabitants, because they have kept it up through all the years since.

In 1971, Long Bow undertook another civic improvement. All the privies built along the streets, in anticipation of a contribution to the family store of fertilizer from anyone passing by, were removed. Now all privies are hidden away in courtyards, and ever since the brigade built its own cement plant, the deep cisterns are covered with concrete slabs that discourage flies, or at least the fly maggots down below. The latter require more fresh air than can circulate under a concrete cover, even one with a slot in it. This improvement has won Long Bow a citation for excellence in public health. But while the concrete slabs have certainly improved sanitation, they have not entirely done away with the background odor of night soil that is characteristic of the whole Chinese countryside—and is in part responsible for that welcome sense of déjà vu that overwhelms one on returning.

Of the famous Dazhai Brigade, high on Tigerhead Mountain, people said:

> High mountains, rock-strewn
>   slopes,
> Step out the door, start
>   climbing up or down.

The popular rhyme about Long Bow stressed the opposite natural features:

Flat land, high watertable,
Step out the door, walk five
li without interruption.

Yet somehow, Dazhai peasants managed to harvest over 100 bushels of grain per acre, while for many years, Long Bow peasants failed to harvest even 30. Even though Mao said that "irrigation is the lifeblood of agriculture," Long Bow peasants failed to make use of their ample water supplies. Every winter the higher authorities mobilized Long Bow for a big effort to prepare the land for more water, and every spring it became clear that very little had been done. The authorities lost patience with this sluggish community and labeled Long Bow an "old, big, difficult place."

The real reason for this sluggishness was the character of Long Bow soil. The more the peasants watered the land, the more intractable it became. Water brought up salt instead of washing it down. When the sun dried the water out, the land cracked into small squares, tearing apart the roots of young plants. The people voted with their feet against irrigation, despairing of ever producing bumper crops, and turned their attention to sidelines, contract work in nearby industries, and even speculation.

A notorious example of local entrepreneurship was Li Hongchang, a bachelor who used to ride freight trains into Hunan province, where he bought dried sweet potatoes that he swapped pound for pound for wheat back in Long Bow; then he sold the wheat for twice what the sweet potatoes had cost him. A four-day trip to Hunan brought in more cash than a month's work in the field.

Hard work to transform the land was further inhibited by changes in ownership. Long Bow had already lost more than one third of its acreage to the railroad, the city-owned cement plant and the saw-blade works. The brigade was compensated for the loss of land by cash payments equal in value to three years of crops, but the saw-blade plant ruined an irrigation project, imposed from above, on which the peasants had expended tens of thousands of labor-days. That labor was never repaid.

The Taihang Saw Blade Works moved to Long Bow from coastal Tianjin in the early 1960s. The educated youth in the village, ninety strong in 1977 but reduced to a handful by 1979 as the authorities stopped sending city dwellers to the countryside, were evenly divided between young men and women. Almost all of them came from Saw Blade, as they called it. They regarded themselves as big-city, Tianjin people, even though most of them had grown up only a few hundred yards from Long Bow. Their contribution to the life of the village was deep and many-faceted. There were science majors, musicians, actors, dancers, artists, and athletes among them. They painted the huge murals that enlivened Long Bow's walls, created the skits that mocked the gang of four during the Army Day celebrations on August 1, and made up at least half of the research group that eventually helped discover how to overcome the alkalinity of Long Bow's soil.

The educated youth, with their Tianjin ways, are only one of many outside influences that have transformed the social life of Long Bow in the past decade. Between the highway and the railroad tracks, temporary reed-and-adobe shelters house tens of thousands of temporary residents—the workers who have come to build a new east-west railroad and their dependents. The overflow from their hastily constructed camp floods Long Bow, and almost every family has one or two groups of outsiders living in its courtyard. There are Korean minority people from Jilin province, coal miners from Fuxun and mechanics from Kailan. Many of them have worked on railroad construction in Africa and have brought home radios, tape recorders, and hand calculators that cannot be bought anywhere in China.

These tenants wear clothes, display hair styles, sing tunes, and use words different from those that Long Bow people are used to. Close contact with them has changed local customs in inconspicuous ways that add up. After a few years of this, Long Bow people find themselves already quite up-to-date compared with peasants who live only a few miles from the railroad, in what the initiated have come to regard as backcountry.

One result of the new sophistication is that Long Bow leaders find it increasingly hard to hold meetings, because there is always a play being performed or a film being shown nearby. These films may be spy thrillers, historical dramas about events before the 1950s, romances in which boy meets girl on a construction project, or foreign films from Vietnam, Korea, and Yugoslavia. Watching these movies has become a habit that has had a devastating effect on other forms of cultural and political life. Some Long Bow children have even decided to reject the expanded local school. The brigade leader's daughter, entirely on her own, transferred to the school run by the Construction Headquarters for railroad workers' children. Her father beat her until his arms tired, but she refused to transfer back.

It is now all but impossible to marry a Long Bow girl unless one is willing to move into Long Bow, because the sophisticated young women there will not leave home, certainly not for any village without quarter-hourly bus service to Changzhi City and twice-daily train service to Zhengzhou and Beijing.

In principle, young people in rural China have a free choice in marriage, but in practice, this is very difficult to achieve because there are so few opportunities for young people to meet. Since most people in the home community are related, one must ordinarily meet someone outside before courtship can begin. Those who don't go away to school or to work in a factory have no chance to meet eligible partners and must rely on parental matchmaking.

But Long Bow is unusually heterogeneous, and young people can sometimes meet and marry inside the village. One who did so in spite of going away to school is Li Lingchiao, a stunning young woman with braids down her back that fall all the way to her waist (at least they did until she cut them off in 1978). Her lips are so formed that they are almost always open, making her seem eager, even slightly breathless. She is vice-leader of the women's association and a member of the brigade's Community Party branch. As a communist, she should have waited until she was twenty-five to marry, and her husband should have waited until he was twenty-eight. But she was married at the age of twenty to a young man of the same age who had been her classmate in the middle school run by the commune at Horse Square, one mile to the north.

She blushed when I asked her about this but explained that her husband's father had been very ill and wanted his son to get married before he died. She didn't want to break the rules, but he was so miserable that she was consumed by pity and agreed to marry the young man. His father, she told me, jumped up from his pallet after that and hasn't been sick a day since.

"But how did you get a license? You were not really old enough."

"We didn't go to our commune office in Horse Square. We went east to Congdao commune. They didn't care. When the gang of four were riding high, administration everywhere just broke down."

If meeting nonrelated young people was the essential condition for free choice in marriage, the educated youth in Long Bow were in an enviable situation. They all lived together in a large two-story building on the site once occupied by the North Temple—men on the ground floor, women upstairs. Yet there were no signs whatsoever of any attachments between them. I asked a delegation that came to talk to me point-blank: "Living here in this dormitory and working together, don't you ever fall in love?"

They all blushed. They all denied that any such thought had ever crossed their minds. They all said that they were too young to be thinking about such things as love and marriage, and even though I pressed them very hard, I could not break this solid front.

Chang was an ex-soldier from Hunan who was assigned to watch the gate of the old brigade headquarters after it was converted into a guesthouse for foreigners. He began almost every conversation with the phrase "I have discovered," and his discoveries almost always turned out to be worth investigating.

"I have discovered," he said to me one day, "that there are still a few hates here."

What he meant by "hates" were hard feelings left over from the Cultural Revolution that began in 1966 and ended sometime between 1970 and 1976, depending on whom you asked. The wounds inflicted by years of bitter factional conflict over who should hold power in the community had been slow to heal.

In the evening, Chang and I used to go outside the gate of the compound and squat in the street, peasant-style, to watch the passing scene. Chang owned a raucous little portable radio that had cost him 13 yuan ($8). He always turned it to Hunan opera, which was broadcast from somewhere south of the border—Shanxi's provincial border. As Long Bow people came down the street, some of them would stop to listen and then to talk.

One night an older man began to curse out the notorious "Little" Li Hongen, who had led the people of the south end of the village when they seized power in 1967. Seizing power meant occupying the brigade office and taking over the official seals. With seals in hand, one could stamp brigade documents, making them official. Above all, one could spend brigade money.

Little Li was a communist of the older generation who backed the young people of Stormy Petrel and Shanggan Ridge, two mass organizations modeled on the student Red Guards who were agitating for power all over the country that year.

When the Stormy Petrel (named after the bird in Gorki's poem "Song of the Stormy Petrel") and Shanggan Ridge (named after a battle in the Korean war) cadres took over the brigade office, they overthrew Shi Shuangguei, the party secretary, and his younger brother, Wang Jinhong, the party vice-secretary. But the rebels couldn't hold on to their power. Most people refused to carry out their orders. After about a week, they were forced to turn the seals over to the Takeover Committee, set up by five other hastily assembled village organizations with names like Truth Fighting Team and Expose Schemes Battle Corps. Within a month power was turned back to Wang as the new party secretary.

To consolidate their power, it was necessary for the five "loyalist" groups to put the "rebels" down and keep them down. They had to make the rebels and their ancestors stink to high heaven, forever. Little Li and the leaders of Stormy Petrel and Shanggan Ridge were denounced as "landlords, rich peasants, counterrevolutionaries and bad elements" who were trying to "reverse the case" on land reform and bring back feudalism. They were arrested, beaten, and driven out of the village. When they ran out of grain, grain coupons, and the hospitality of relatives in outlying counties, they returned to Long Bow, only to be arrested, beaten, and driven out again. It was late 1969 before they were able to come home and stay home, and late 1971 before the label "counterrevolutionary" was officially removed from the record. By that time, the charges had penetrated so deeply into the popular consciousness that they could not easily be erased. Years later, an old man on the street could still curse Little Li for trying to "reverse the case" on land reform.

The first person killed in the Cultural Revolution in Shanxi died on the threshing floor of Long Bow's Fourth Production Team. He was not a Long Bow Brigade member but a student at the Luan middle school, housed at that time on the grounds of the old Catholic orphanage. He had come with members of his faction to raid the school for the grain and grain tickets needed for subsistence. He was killed by a random bullet fired by a railroad worker when the grain raid escalated into a night battle for control of the railroad yards.

"When I think about it, it frightens me," said Wang Jinhong, now chairman but no longer party secretary of the Long Bow Brigade. "In the struggle here, we could easily have killed someone. Brigade members could have died just as that student did. We were lucky. Things never went that far, but it scares me to think about it."

"Do you really think that the rebels were 'landlords, rich peasants, counterrevolutionaries, and bad elements?'" I asked.

"I don't now, but I did then. We convinced ourselves of it. The wind of denunciation was blowing through the whole region. Everybody thought their opposition was counterrevolutionary."

Wang Jinhong has been in and out of local office so often that his career resembles that of Vice-Premier Deng Xiaoping at the national level. Since 1966, he has been twice overthrown and three times elevated to top posts in the brigade. Physicaly, Jinhong stands out because of his massive forehead and the fact that he is slightly hunchbacked. He carried loads that were too heavy for him when he was little, and the carrying pole bent his back and thrust his head permanently forward. This makes him look, when he walks, as if he cannot wait to get where he is going and is searching somewhat anxiously for a quicker way to his goal. This impression matches his true character. Jinhong is indeed eager, inquisitive, impatient—and very smart.

After he came back to power as party secretary in 1967, he led the village through the last years of the Cultural Revolution. Later, he was held responsible for the factional excesses that had shattered unity and undermined production. But he was caught up in events that no one could control. How could a brigade leader be blamed when the People's Liberation Army general, who was charged with reconciling the factions in the region, instead framed the civilian who was his rival for the top post, calling him a Kuomintang agent?

Whatever his share of the blame, Wang Jinhong was removed from office in 1971 by a work team sent from Changzhi City to try and straighten out the tangle left behind by the Cultural Revolution. Frustrated and depressed by the sudden "reversal of case" that led to the rehabilitation of his arch-opponent. Little Li, Jinhong, and several associates ran away. But as Little Li had discovered when he was on the run, there was no place that a peasant without a ration book could go. After a few days, Jinhong returned home. For a while, he earned a living building houses for neighborhood families; then he agreed to manage a little repair shop for bicycles, handcarts, donkey carts, and tractor wagons that the brigade had set up beside the road. The shop prospered due to Jinhong's skills, at a time when other brigade production continued to stagnate. The work team took to calling Jinhong and his friends the Black Gang because they refused to bow their heads when they passed through the village. Proud of the label, the Black Gang stuck together, shared such things as the piglets from Jinhong's fertile sow, defied the rest of the community, and effectively undermined the authority of the group then in charge at brigade headquarters.

The fact of the matter was that Jinhong was technically the most skillful and politically the most farsighted man in Long Bow. He had been recruited as an apprentice electrician in 1958 and had spent four years as a power plant construction worker on projects all over north China—years that served him as a "university." He had learned enough about electrical wiring, welding, engine repair, and building design to support himself in any of these trades. And he had also learned some political economy. Most of the young people in the brigade looked to Jinhong for leadership, whether he was in office or out. When he was out, they lost interest in politics and tried to learn from him some of the technical skills he had acquired.

Finally, in 1973, Wang Jinhong was restored to office. He criticized himself, accepted some responsibility for the factionalism of the 1960s, and vowed to unite with others to change things in Long Bow. That was the turning point. Wang Jinhong and the leaders who had temporarily replaced him put their differences aside and concentrated on making some sort of breakthrough in production. That they succeeded is illustrated by the steady rise in grain yields from 28 bushels per acre in 1970, the approximate level for the previous twenty years, to 48 bushels in 1973, then 60 in 1974, and 100 in 1979.

I was fascinated by this sudden leap in production. Obviously it had awaited a political settlement that could unite the brigade. But once the brigade united, there was still the technical question—how had the problem of the alkalinity of Long Bow's soil been overcome?

"Ever since we lost so much land to industry," Jinhong said, "we have been growing more and more market vegetables. To make them grow, we get the night soil, the kitchen waste and the ashes from the workers' homes. We found that when we put a lot of coal ashes on the soil, the salt receded. It got washed down, not sucked up.

"Then we noticed something strange," he continued. "At the power plant near Yellow Mill, the great chimney threw ashes all over the countryside. People protested, but the plant managers did nothing. In a circle around the plant, the crops all turned gray. But every year, they grew better than the year before. It was the ashes. They did something to the heavy clay. They increased the percolation.

"So we put the schoolchildren to work at an experiment supervised by Shen Majin's research group. They hauled ashes from the waste pile at the power plant and put them on their experimental plot, over 100 tons to the acre. We covered the land three to four inches deep. It worked. The yields almost doubled. So after that, we put all the production teams to work hauling ashes. Each year, each team converted some of its land.

"Once the land was converted, we could irrigate. We had to dig more wells, pump more water, divert more water from the reservoir, fix up irrigation channels and level the land. That took a lot of labor. Our best people used to be out earning money at various jobs—unloading freight at the railroad station, cutting steel bars at the steel mill, hauling rock by handcart for the cement mill. We had to call them all home.

"For the first time in twenty years, we put agriculture in first place, and it really paid off."

"Your sidelines seem to be flourishing, too," I said.

"Well, we concentrated on sidelines that could use partial labor power—like the teenage girls. They are polishing the saw blades and making the saw handles for the saw-blade works. We needed wood for the saw handles, so we bought a sawmill. Of course, that takes skilled people. We needed phosphate fertilizer, but we found we could only buy the raw rock. So we set up a grinding mill. Then we converted it into a cement plant. With some of that output, we can supply the raw material for lining our irrigation canals. All these projects are very profitable, much more so than the wages we used to earn outside. Twelve percent of our labor power working at sidelines now produces seventy percent of our income."

Wang Jinhong, the brigade chairman, can enjoy play as well as work, tradition as well as change. For example, he joined the Long Bow village stilt dancers when the people went to Changzih City to celebrate the conclusion of a national party congress. For the occasion, Jinhong was made up as a young bride riding home on a donkey to visit her mother. A papier-mâché donkey's neck and head protruded from his stomach, while matching rear and tail extended from his backside, and he leaped in response to a whip wielded by a colleague made up as a donkey driver. Another mock maiden dangled a butterfly from a string on the end of a fish pole while her symbolic suitor tried vainly to catch it. Still other stilt walkers portrayed Liberation Army soldiers, maidens of the minority nationalities, peasants, workers, and the political target of the times—the gang of four, under whose influence stilts had been banned in Long Bow for years.

Stilts are a very old tradition in Shanxi Province, but only Long bow has stilt dancers who do acrobatics, jump over tables, and climb up and down ramps. The village learned this kind of stilt walking from a captured Kuomintang officer who was "reeducated" there in 1945, when the Communists' famous Resistance University, headed by Lin Biao, migrated to Long Bow from Yan'an.

The dancers stood so tall on their stilts that even the shortest of them looked down on the musicians playing on the high, jolting bed of a four-wheeled trailer drawn through the city streets by tractor. The horn player's cheeks puffed out like two swollen bladders. His fingers moved so swiftly that they blurred. Sometimes he held the horn away from his face and blew through the reed alone. This sounded like two turkeys in a forest squaring off for battle. The bamboo pipes, the snakeskin fiddles, and the bulging red drums of the other performers fell silent to let the turkeys quarrel, then suddenly resumed their frantic rhythm as the horn, two octaves lower now, rejoined its reed.

The music trailer, with its long double line of elevated dancers, moved slowly down the city streets through dense crowds of celebrants. Ahead and behind it moved other floats, other performers, other dancers, and acrobats, some of them also on stilts, in what seemed to be an endless procession. Their motion on the street generated a dense cloud of dust that softened all outlines. Through the dust, one could look ahead to see villagers holding costumed children high overhead on flexible poles, and behind to see factory workers dip and roll various huge papier-mâché figures. A second trailer carried a pyramid of opera stars made up to resemble the heroes of Water Margin, the men driven onto Liang Mountain in the days of the Sung Dynasty, eight centuries ago. This was the first time these legendary figures had appeared in public for ten years.

China's most persistent tradition is tilling the land by hoe.

We were all out in the fields wielding our heavy, mattocklike hoes. Smash. Drive the blade in, pull the soil back, break the biggest lumps. Smash, drive the blade in again . . . try not to take any extra steps, they compact the soil.

"How long is it going to be?" asked Jinhong.

"How long is what going to be?"

"This bit with the hoe! We're stuck here with hoes in our hands one thousand, two thousand, three thousand years. It's time to get rid of these jewels."

"That it is," I said.

"I'm not afraid of hard work. I'm willing to hoe alongside the next man. But I don't like it. In America you till 250 acres alone. I'm lucky if I till one. It's time for a change!"

"It's hard to run a tractor through a field when you have two crops growing together."

"Never mind two crops. We'll plant corn alone until we learn to do it with machines. And we'll push up yields while we do it."

"Do you mean that?"

"Yes."

"What will the commune say?"

"That's a problem. When you try things in America, you take a chance. If you fail, you can't pay back your crop loan. You risk your land. There is no such risk here, but I still can't try out most things to the point of finding out if they succeed or fail. The way it has been here the past few years, the commune has decided everything—what to plant, where to plant it, what variety, how much seed, how deep, how far apart. If you try anything new, they come down hard right away.

'What are you trying to do? Set up your own Central Committee?' The technical question turns into a political question. You are violating democratic centralism."

"That makes it hard. How can you experiment with anything?"

"It isn't easy. But really, here in the brigade we are in a better position than anyone else to try things. Take mechanization. We have land, labor power, money, and materials. What materials we don't have, we can usually find. Who else has that kind of leverage? The supply departments have materials, but no labor power. The factories have labor power but no materials. The mechanization office has nothing but a sign on the door. What can those fellows do but talk?"

Wang Jinhong was not content with mere talk. He went ahead on his own without regard to the consequences. In 1977, he asked me such questions as, How would you put grain on the second floor of the office building? How would you irrigate corn land? How would you dry grain? I suggested a grain auger, a center-pivot irrigation system, and a coal-fired grain drier. (A grain auger is like a long, unbroken screw or drill bit that carries grain up the spiral formed by its turning threads. A center-pivot irrigation system is a pipe up to half a mile long, mounted on wheels every few yards; it turns in a huge circle around a well at the center, which provides water for the pipe to spray at intervals up to the outer circumference.)

Instead of saying, as so many in China are wont to do, "Someday we'll have those things," Jinhong said, "I'm going to start tomorrow." In ten days, he built a grain auger twenty-six feet long. In a month, he built a center-pivot irrigation pipe 100 yards long that traveled full circle under its own power. Over the winter, he built a grain drier that broke through all the obstacles that had plagued grain handling in the brigade for years.

Then in 1979, he launched a 100-acre experiment in the mechanization of corn farming. With some equipment borrowed from the Mechanization Institute of the province, with other equipment built in Long Bow, and with support and advice from various levels of the government, his special team produced over twenty-five tons of grain per worker, a fourteen fold increase in productivity in one year.

This achievement had extraordinary implications. It meant that for every person left raising crops, fourteen could leave the land and do something else. In Long Bow, they could probably be absorbed manufacturing grain augers, irrigation systems and grain driers—if the state supported the idea with the necessary supplies.

That was a big "if." My impression was that China's leaders had not yet confronted the question of the mechanization of peasant agriculture. Or if they had, they had backed away from it. Combines for the wastelands of the Northeast and Xinjiang—yes. Milking machines for state-operated dairies—yes. But corn planters, corn pickers, and herbicides for Shanxi villages—well, maybe, probably not. The upheaval this would cause in the economy staggered the imagination. There was no commitment to any program that could accomplish it. In fact, the thrust of much public argument was against it. The status quo of the hoe was defended with the slogan: no mechanization for mechanization's sake.

Nevertheless, in the fall of 1978, the government did take concrete steps to untie the hands of peasant innovators. Beijing announced that state functionaries must respect the property rights of cooperative units. Within the framework of some general guidelines, production brigades and teams had the right to make their own management decisions, to grow what suited them best in a manner that reflected local conditions. If implemented, this decision could liberate enormous creative forces. One could only hope they would not be blocked by some new countercurrent of bureaucratic obstruction.

Jinhong had been sick for three days. Since nothing seemed to be happening on the street and nobody came or went through the big door of the brigade office except the accountant, we decided to go and find out where all the action had gone. Gatekeeper Zhang and I followed the only person who seemed to be heading anywhere. His trail led straight to Jinhong's home.

The main section of the house was ample in size. There was a low-ceilinged living room about 15 feet long, then a doorway leading to a dimly lit bedroom on the east. The main room was full of people, about ten in all, and there were two more in the bedroom talking to Jinhong, who was lying fully dressed on a wide wooden bed. Manfu, the opera lover from the saw-blade shop, lean Chou-fa covered with grime after a twelve-hour shift in the cement mill, Wende from the Fifth Team garden, reeking of raw pig manure, two capped and jacketed buyers from a trading organization in the city, and a messenger from Horse

Square Commune milled about, waiting their turn and all talking at once. In the cookhouse outside, Dr. Shen of the brigade clinic was brewing a special cough medicine out of herbs. He had to compete for space on the adobe stove with Jinhong's willful daughter, who was heating some gruel for her father.

When the two men in the bedroom came out—they were leaders of a neighboring brigade—the two buyers went in. As they ducked through the door, each pulled a pack of cigarettes from his pocket. It was a conditioned reflex. Prior to doing business, one offered a cigarette.

Seeing this, Chang called me into a corner for a confidential aside. When dealing with certain industrial units and certain notorious functionaries, he said, buyers from the countryside had to be prepared with three kinds of armament—the twenty-shot clip (pack of name-brand cigarettes), the hand grenade (bottle of fine wine), and the explosive satchel (box of sweet biscuits). Working out the terms of a deal had come to be known as *yen chiu, yen chiu*, which means "to study the question"—but also means "cigarettes and wine, cigarettes and wine." Needless to say, Jinhong had no use for any such preliminaries. His policy was to judge each offer on its merits.

While we waited for the buyers to complete their business—they wanted guarantees on a large order of cement—three other people came in. One was a cadre from the Railroad Construction Bureau who wanted to negotiate the transfer of more Long Bow land. The second was the head mechanic from the trucking depot at the railroad yards. He had completed repairs on one of Long Bow's tractors. The last one in was Zhang Wenying, head of the women's association. What she had to announce, with her usual good cheer, was that a delegation of sanitary inspectors was on its way. She wanted people mobilized to sweep the streets. Dr. Shen offered her a cigarette. She lit it from the burned stub already in her mouth.

"Two more women have agreed to have their tubes tied," she said.

"How many does that make altogether?"

"Fifty this year."

It was a commune record.

Jinhong suddenly appeared out of the bedroom, concerned that we had not been offered tea.

"Aren't you supposed to be sick?" I asked.

"Oh, it's not that bad. I'm almost well now," he protested with a voice that faded halfway through the sentence. Then he coughed, a rasping sound that came from deep in his chest. He didn't sound well to me, but no one else seemed worried. The dampness underfoot aggravated coughs, and so did the dust in the air. Within a few hours after every rain, the dust blew up again because so much of the earth was bare. You could feel grit in your mouth whenever you clenched your teeth.

It did Jinhong little good to stay home. The affairs of the brigade followed him day and night. They were ever present, like the dust. But his spirit, if not his body, thrived on the challenge. And I could see why. I had a strong sense, sitting there that day, of the vitality the raw energy, the unleashed creative power of the cooperative and its 2,000 members. There had been years of stagnation. They could be repeated. But right now the sluices were open, and almost everyone was wading out to do battle—remaking the soil, bringing in water, setting up industries, building homes, taking hold of birth control, planning a new school, sending out buyers to places as distant as Shanghai and Harbin. Above all, they had the temerity to challenge the age-old dominance of the hoe. That impressed me the most.

大 A Trip
回 to
潮 Fengyang County, 1983

"When have peasants ever dreamed of owning two-story houses? Out here on the upper veranda we can sit outside in the evening and forget about mosquito bites. In all history there hasn't been anything like this. I support the new policy with all my heart. May it last forever!"

So said former poor peasant and ex-beggar, Yang Jingli. Every time we asked him a simple question his words soared skyward in oratorical flights of praise for the "responsibility system." He could hardly focus his thoughts on such mundane matters as yield per acre or the price of a fat pig.

I could understand Yang's enthusiasm. Houyang, the tiny hamlet he called home, had long been notorious as a disaster area. In 1979 its male inhabitants, traditionally so poor that they could not attract brides, included seventeen bachelors. Although they farmed six times as much land per capita as most peasants in China, isolation in a far corner of their home county, incompetent leadership, and recurring natural disasters had driven them out onto the highways to search for alms season after season. Now, four years after disbanding collective labor in favor of family-oriented land contracts, the more skillful husbandmen among them had doubled, tripled, even quadrupled their grain production. More than half the bachelors had already found wives and several ex-beggars had paid cash for concrete-block, tile-roofed, two-story homes that dwarfed the trees round about.

This article originally appeared in *Monthly Review* 35, no. 6 (November 1983).

Houyang is one of the showplaces of Fengyang county, the rural backwater that Vice-Premier Wan Li set on a new course in 1979. Since then this hamlet and many of its neighboring communities have enjoyed rising prosperity. Countywide grain production has gone up by 50,000 long tons a year to reach levels 100 percent above all previous records. Public warehouses overflow with rice, wheat, soybeans, and oil seeds that the overburdened railroads cannot move out. Stimulated by these abundant supplies, new processing industries are growing apace, financed by individual peasant investors who have both money and time on their hands.

I went to Fengyang county in March 1983 to see the best that the new contract system, now all but mandatory in China, had to offer. In a 1981 meeting with Vice-Premier Wan Li I had expressed grave doubts about the wisdom of breaking up collective lands and especially those lands that were already well farmed by competently led, prosperous cooperators. Whereas Central Committee policy statements called for a selective policy, recommending family contracts only where collective management had failed, Shanxi province peasants to whom I had talked said the pressure on all collectives, good or bad, had been relentless. Party leaders were demanding break-up regardless of the circumstances, an all-or-nothing thrust that people called "one stroke of the knife." Wan Li hotly denied that this was the policy at the Central Committee level. "The people are free to choose," he insisted. He nevertheless recommended that I go and take a look at what the contract system had created in Anhui province. Two years later, just as my old friends in Long Bow village finally bowed to extreme pressure and broke up what had developed into one of the most advanced joint farming efforts in China, I finally found the time to travel southward and have a look at what the future might hold in store.

The first thing that struck me while driving north from the provincial capital, Hefei, was the extreme backwardness of the North Anhui countryside. We seemed to have slipped in time toward the middle ages—abandoned irrigation works led to clusters of crumbling adobe huts whose age-blackened thatch roofs topped frameless window and door openings. Mud-clogged yards rose only slightly above the level of the stagnant puddles in the street. Swaybacked pigs, lean and worm laden, wandered aimlessly between gangs of restless, unwashed children. Only the clothing on the backs of the latter belied the general impression of abject poverty. Boys and girls ran about, not in preliberation-style rags, but in fairly well made jackets and pants of printed machine woven cloth. Numerous as they were, the children on the streets were heavily outnumbered by the scores of loitering adults who seemed to have nothing but time on their hands—the leisure time that is the curse of every backward countryside in the world.

Production figures for the years before 1979 documented the economic stagnation that underlay the poverty and chronic underemployment we saw all around us. For more than twenty years yields had remained at or below 30 bushels to the acre and per capita gain production in 1977 (1978 was a disastrous drought year) had fallen below that of 1952. Here was a region where for whatever reason cooperation had failed. After two decades of social experimentation the peasants of North Anhui had nowhere to go but up.

I could only conclude that Fengyang had suffered atrocious leadership in the past. County leaders told me that none of the cooperative policies seemed to work. Local cadres beat their heads against a stone wall of apathy and people on the land dragged their feet in defiance of their own best interests. Yields, after all, depended on sustained local effort. Why should the people with the most to gain do nothing or next to nothing to ensure them?

Deputy County Chairman Wang Changtai said it was because the link between the effort put out by any given individual and the reward obtained was too tenuous. Peasants simply could not visualize any improvement coming to them personally through hard work. Their goal was to do as little as possible and depend on the state to carry everyone through until spring. When bad weather undermined their meager efforts even the state could not fill the gap. Tens of thousands went out to beg. Wang said that in the past natural disasters—either droughts or floods—struck nine years out of ten. On the average 50,000 left home to beg every winter. In the worst years 150,000 went out. Those who went out didn't always come back. Among the males who came back many never found wives. The population grew slowly. In some places it even declined—a phenomenon that helped set the stage for the success of the new policy. When the time came to divide the land each person got at least 2 mou (⅓ acre) while some got as many as

.5 (almost 1 acre). This was from two to five times the national average and provided a relatively secure base for family-style production.

I found it difficult to understand why cooperation should fail so dismally in Anhui while succeeding so well in many other places that I had visited over the years. A 1980 national survey made by a group of young economists that included the newly appointed second secretary of the Fengyang Party Committee, Wong Yongxi, conduded that in China as a whole 30 percent of the cooperative brigades had been doing well, 30 percent had been doing badly, while in the middle 40 percent had been holding their own, neither chalking up great successes on the one hand nor floundering on the other. Most, though not all, of the successful cooperatives that I had seen were in the north, in or near old liberated areas where the peasants first gave support to the Communist Party because it led the resistance war against Japan or the liberation war against the Guomindang. Years of armed struggle had developed a core of politically aware peasant cadres who later led the land reform and the cooperative movement, and led both fairly well, in many localities at least. Anhui, on the other hand, had gone through no such history. Liberated by northern armies in 1949, Anhui went through land reform under outside leadership in 1952, then without any trial period of mutual aid, plunged into a land-pooling movement that leaped from the lower to the higher stage in the course of a few months. In the lower stage land shares counted when distributing income, in the higher stage only labor counted. Before the latter could even pretend to achieve consolidation the commune movement carried egalitarianism to unprecedented extremes. Joint tillage never recovered prestige.

According to Wang Yongxi the cooperative movement in Anhui violated two fundamental principles of rural organization: the principle that peasant participation must be voluntary, based on the economic success of local models, and the principle that income must be distributed on the basis of work performed. Party leaders, ignoring these fundamentals, rushed the peasants into advanced levels of cooperation before they saw any convincing evidence of advantages to be gained and set up forms of income distribution that divided earnings more or less equally per capita, without regard for individual effort expended. Inexperienced local leaders, unable to generate any production enthusiasm under the new share-and-share-alike system, ended up using their power to feather their own nests. Periodically those who exposed, challenged, and replaced them, when faced with the same inertia, ended up applying the same values and began to serve themselves rather than the community. When thirty years after liberation Anhui peasants failed to generate levels of per capita production any higher than those with which they started out, men like the current first secretary of the Party Committee, Wang Yuxin, his deputy Song Linsheng, and Deputy County Chairman Wang Changtai decided it was time for an agonizing reappraisal, time to reverse course.

Wang Yuxin said the decision took courage because what they decided to try out was a variant of Liu Shoaqi's notorious "Three Freedoms, One Contract," a policy denounced over the years as "capitalist road." Wang and his colleagues introduced it in two stages. First they urged the peasants to split their production teams into small groups, each one of which then contracted to grow crops on designated plots of land. When this brought some positive results in 1979, the leaders urged the peasants to go further and contract land family by family according to a system that they called "Da Bao Gan" (the all-inclusive contract). Da Bao Gan can best be described as "render unto Caesar that which is Caesar's while I take the rest for myself."

Fengyang peasants, frustrated by what they came to look on as their cooperative straitjacket, wanted an average per capita share of land to work, but they did not want production quotas, percentage bonuses, sliding-scale obligations. They wanted to know what the government, the public sector, absolutely had to have from the land in the way of cash and kind. Then they promised to deliver this minimum without question just so long as they could do what they pleased with the balance of their crops.

Secretary Wang went along with this. At the provincial level Wan Li backed him up, and so the "responsibility system," in the form of the all-inclusive contract, was born. In Fengyang county, where there is more land per capita than almost anywhere else in China, each family got on the average the use of 2 mou (⅓ acre) of land per person. In return for this each promised to pay its national agricultural tax in kind, to turn over a small sum for the support of local (brigade and commune) officials, and to sell to the state at established prices the low fixed quotas of grain that tradition had set for every mou. This arrangement, because it demanded relatively little, unleashed the energy and enthusiasm of the peasnts and pushed production ahead in striking fashion. Overall grain production figures for the county showed a steady rise:

1977	180,000	long tons
1978 (drought).	147,500	" "
1979 (group contracts)	220,000	" "
1980 (family contracts)	251,000	" "
1981 (family contracts)	320,000	" "
1982 (family contracts)	359,000	" "

"I thought we would get results with this system," said Secretary Wang, "but I never thought the results would be so striking and so sustained. It has been a surprise to me, it has been a surprise to everyone."

During each crop season after 1979 the peasants got up earlier, worked harder, stayed longer in the fields than before and they accomplished each day much more than they ever had since pooling their land in 1956. As a result they finished off most of each year's work in a few intense months, then stood idle for the remainder of the season. "In our cooperative days," said Yang Chiangli, "we used to work all day, every day, year-in and year-out, but we got almost nothing done—work a little, take a break, work a little more, take another break. We felt harassed and we produced very little. What we were doing looked like work but in fact we were stalling around. Now we make every minute count. Our labor produces results. We earn a good living and we have time on our hands, lots of time."

With Deputy County Chairman Wang Changtai's help I examined several household accounts in detail. Here are the figures for Li Wanhua of Zhanglaozhuang team, Zhanglaozhuang brigade, Ershihying commune:

With eight people in the family Li contracted 22.5 mou or 2.8 mou per person (slightly under ½ acre apiece). According to his contract for 1982 he obligated himself to pay 91.74 yuan into the team accumulation fund (to pay local cadres' salaries, supply welfare to needy families, etc.), to turn over 545 catties (11 bushels) of grain to the state as his agricultural tax, and to sell 679 catties (13.5 bushels) of quota grain to the state at normal state grain prices. Over and above that he planned to sell 2,392 catties (47.84 bushels) of above-quota grain to the state at prices 50 percent above normal, and to sell 25.5 catties of vegetable oil, 498 catties of dried tobacco, 2 fat pigs, and 10 catties of fresh eggs. His actual production far surpassed the above plan and he ended the year with 20,300 catties (406 bushels) of grain, 960 catties of tobacco, 600 catties of oil seeds (mostly sesame), and 800 catties (15 bushels) of soybeans, not to mention the returns from such sidelines as pig and poultry raising. His net income from all sources reached 4,800 yuan or 600 yuan per capita, almost twice the county average. Prior to 1979, before contracting began, Li never accumulated enough work points to pay for the family's per capita grain at 520 catties per head supplied by the brigade. He always had to make up the difference by turning over the income realized from the sale of his two pigs. Cash income retained came to less than 100 yuan per person. Li insisted that in those days the family got along, but quite clearly its members were "getting along" much better in 1983.

At Yaoyin brigade we met a young married man, Yao Yukuo, who had also previously earned only 500 catties of per capita grain and 100 yuan per person in cash a year. Now, with 5.4 mou (just under 1 acre) contracted he and his wife each enjoyed a net income in cash and kind worth 700 yuan, and this after paying taxes that amounted to 20 yuan in cash to the local accumulation fund and 300 catties of grain (worth 60 yuan) for the state. Yao insisted that he worked only about four months out of every year and thoroughly enjoyed the long winter slack. As we talked we sat in his new stone and tile house (stone walls, fired tile roof). Since he had cut the stone himself the house cost him only 3,000 yuan, a sum he had already paid in full.

Most prosperous of all the peasants we met was old Yang Changli, the former beggar from Houyang, who so annoyed us with his oratory. In 1982 he contracted 42 mou (7 acres) for eight people and harvested:

wheat	270 bushels	
rice	324 "	
soybeans	47 "	
grain sorghum	12 "	
sweet potatoes	61 "	(grain equivalent)
edible beans	12 "	

After winning 10 bushels of grain as a prize for his record-shattering production Yang's total grain holdings reached 726 bushels, or more than 20 long tons. In addition he harvested tobacco (2,000 catties), peanuts (1,000 catties), rape seed (400 catties), hemp seed (50 catties), mint oil (20 catties). With his surplus grain and screenings he fed three fat pigs, sixteen suckling pigs, thirty ducks, and twenty-nine chickens. Both ducks and chickens laid eggs which he sold for cash.

Yang's net income, after deducting all costs including taxes, topped 10,000 yuan, for a per capita income of 1,250 yuan. Rich beyond his wildest dreams he plunked down 6,000 yuan cash for his new two-story house, then bought three Shanghai bicycles and a sewing machine on the side.

The three families described above were doing better than most. All of them surpassed the county average for per capita income by 100 percent or more. But the average per capita income in the county had doubled in four years' time and signs of this sharp increase made themselves evident everywhere. Most conspicuous were the many new houses built by individual families, the enormous new enclosed theaters built by communes, the bulging warehouses at the state grain stations, and the lively buying and selling at the rotating farm markets. Deputy County Chairman Wang liked to stress less conspicuous things like the 5 million yuan annual increase in private productive capital— tools, machines, carts, and work buffalo; the sharp annual increase in peasant-owned bicycles, sewing machines, watches, and radios. Collective productive capital showed a parallel rise, pyramiding at the rate of 1 million yuan a year, the most conspicuous addition here being the 500 kilometers of power line built in four years, an amount equal to the total kilometers previously built. Each community not yet provided with power made a per capita assessment for this purpose. Everyone in Houyang had contributed 15 yuan. Concrete poles, ready for erection, lay along the road to the county seat. The road itself was new and had also been built by subscription.

Houyang's Yang Chingli boasted that he meant to concentrate on grain production and break all his old production records in the years to come. It seemed obvious, however, that in the realm of grain Fengyang county was approaching a plateau. With over 60 bushels of wheat and over 100 bushels of rice per acre unit yields were pushing the limits set by the state of the art. If incomes were to continue to rise expanded livestock production, other rural sidelines, and many small industries must soon make their appearance. That also seemed the only way to employ the thousands who were idling away their winters without gainful employment.

For promising examples of sidelines production Deputy County Chairman Wang took us to see Gaojen commune. There 7,300 able-bodied laborers farmed 31,875 mou, an average of 4.5 (over ⅔ of an acre) per person. Since one man or woman to every 10 mou would be enough, commune head Li figured that he had 3,500 too many workers on the land and was busy encouraging the establishment of every possible sideline. So far Gaojen people had set up eighty-three enterprises that employed some 2,500 people while more than 1,000 still remained jobless. Families started most of the enterprises, three to eight households joining up, pooling capital, and going into the production of such things as cement blocks, clay tiles, asbestos tiles, fired brick, phosphate fertilizer, fish ponds, flour milling, oil pressing, starch making, and stone crushing. Several had also set up construction companies. Individual families joined brigades and communes to set up a number of larger joint stock companies that financed, among other things, three mechanized stone crushing plants and one medium-sized flour mill.

We went to see the flour mill, capitalized at 41,000 yuan. To build it the commune put up 4.5 mou of land valued at 2,000 yuan and 24 shares of stock valued at 1,000 yuan apiece. Individual families bought 15 shares of stock at 1,000 yuan apiece. Each share of stock bought by a family carried with it a full-time job in the plant plus one full vote at the shareholders meeting of seventeen (fifteen workers, one delegate from the commune, and one delegate from the local team). The meeting chose a management committee of three, which in turn hired a manager. During the last eight months of 1982 the flour mill turned a net profit of 10,812 yuan, distributed 23 percent as dividends and put the balance into an accumulation fund destined for new investment. The workers made 58.2 yuan a month in wages plus a year-end bonus of a pair of leather work shoes valued at 17 yuan per pair.

"What are the advantages of such a plant?" asked commune chairman Li. "It provides employment for surplus labor, an outlet for surplus funds, and an opportunity for democratic management. Every worker owns stock and every stockholder has a vote."

This last point was not unimportant. One of the continuing problems with rural cooperatives in China has been one-person rule, the abuse of power allocated from above, in units seen as part of the foundation of the state. These new enterprises, financed from below and outside the state system, are run by those who own them. If the manager does not suit the shareholders, who are also the workers, they fire the manager. When the stockholders of one new stone crushing company were looking for a manager they stipulated that at least 65 yuan a month in wages per worker and 196 yuan in dividends per share per year (30 percent of the anticipated 57,500 net profit) had to be provided. This accomplishment would earn the manager the right to nominate the staff, sign contracts with workers, fire them if they violated their contracts, and receive twice the bonus allocated to each worker. (I forgot to ask how a manager could fire a worker who was also a shareholder.) If on the other hand the manager failed to meet the level of wages and profits stipulated the difference had to be made up out of his or her own pocket. A manager who did not make up the difference faced charges, arrest, and a sojourn in jail!

At Gaojen commune new industries fell far short of providing employment for all. But in a lonely backwater at the opposite end of the county we visited a brigade where due to special circumstances every able-bodied person had full off-season employment. This brigade occupied a site near a big lake where the acreage of reeds almost equaled the acreage of arable land. Each family contracted, in addition to their per capita farm land, some reed land, and the reeds they cut and stored provided year-round work weaving mats. The average worker could weave at lest two mats a day worth 2 yuan apiece wholesale. The constant weaving combined with work on the land brought in the highest average income per capita in the whole county: 900 yuan a year. Here peasant families were building new houses by the dozen, buying bicycles, radios, television sets, and walking tractors. Their village lay way off the beaten track beyond the back of nowhere and seemed to be slowly sinking into the mud of the lake shore, but they displayed high spirits and an enthusiasm for modernization. All the families we talked to had ambitious plans for the future. They were planning two-story houses primarily because they wanted to convert ground floor space into mat-weaving workshops. They expected electricity to arrive within a year. This lakeside community demonstrated the income potential of a well-matched farming/sideline combination and the importance of year-round work as an income booster. Labor power remains China's most abundant resource. The big problem is putting it to work.

Everywhere we went in Fengyang county people talked most about and expected the most from one crop: rice. The newest thing in rice culture was hybrid seed with a yield potential well above 100 bushels per acre. Some brigades were already specializing in hybrid rice seed, which they sold at 2.5 yuan per catty. Rice requires water. At least half the water came from large-scale irrigation works created by the mass movements of the 1950s. The rest came from small lakes, ponds, and catchment basins built locally over many years. Taken together they stored water that could irrigate about one-third of the county's arable land. In contrast to the disarray so evident in the counties to the south, almost all the water works, the canals, the sluices, and the pumps in Fengyang seemed to be in operating condition. Had all this been contracted out along with the land? And if so, how?

Deputy County Chairman Wang assured us that the people still owned the water system collectively. Communes and brigades organized the distribution of water as needed, but in contrast to the past no one got water without advance cash payment. To learn how this system worked we went to the large Fengyashan reservoir on the western edge of the county. There low rolling hills suddenly gave way to two large mountains that provided a perfect dam site. With a water surface of 146 square kilometers the reservoir held some 125 million cubic meters of water, about half of which could be tapped for irrigation. The reservoir was currently supplying water to 89,000 mou (almost 15,000 acres) and stimulating striking increases in the yield of rice. At Yingjian commune, one of five supplied by the reservoir, yields had gone from 51 bushels to the acre in 1978 to 118 bushels to the acre in 1982. Deputy County Chairman Wang said the yields went up after peasants contracted the land out because (1) the peasants worked harder; (2) they bought more fertilizer (four times as much as in 1978); (3) they planted large areas to high-yielding hybrid rice; and (4) they watered every field carefully (paying for every cubic meter in advance made this a necessity).

The reservoir, built by collective labor in the year of the Great Leap Forward, remained a state unit. The staff, hired by the county, was supposed to finance both daily operations and capital improvements through the sale of water and fish, but prior to 1979 neither product yielded much income. When peasant collectives needed water county officials had little choice but to order it released. Recipients promised to pay for it later but very few ever kept their promises. Every year the county had to invest 3,000–4,000 yuan to stock the water with fish but poachers took so many of them that the official annual catch never realized enough cash to pay for the fingerlings.

In 1979 all this changed. First the reservoir staff put irrigation water on a pay-as-you-go basis. Teams, brigades, and communes down below had to collect cash in advance from peasant users at .50 yuan per 100 cubic meters. At the same time they organized a water watch, team-by-team, brigade-by-brigade, to make sure the water reached each locality. The reservoir staff, cash in hand, released enough extra water to cover all losses due to evaporation and seepage and kept up the flow until each family got what it paid for on its home fields. Water revenues went up from 6,000 yuan in 1978 to 49,000 yuan in 1982 and put the reservoir for the first time into the black.

Next the reservoir staff reorganized the fishing industry. The reservoir as a state unit entered into contracts with three nearby communes and five shoreline brigades and sold development shares at 2,000 yuan apiece. The reservoir put in three shares, each commune bought one, and the five brigades together bought one. This brought in enough money to stock the lake with fingerlings. With money of their own invested the local people kept a sharp eye out for poachers, drove off those they discovered (one man drowned trying to escape capture), and shared a fish catch that surpassed 100 tons. At 800–1,000 yuan a ton, each unit received tens of thousands of dollars. Here suddenly they had a sideline worth developing. Manager Chen estimated the potential future catch at 200 tons. Deputy County Chairman Wang thought the total could be pushed to 1,000 tons if only they found ways to feed the fish and stocked species that thrived at different depths on waste material from the segment above.

Our quick survey of the county—four intense days of visits to advanced units north, south, east, and west—revealed a countryside on the move, production, both agricultural and industrial, rising, incomes rising, and the quality of life improving. Everyone attributed the progress to the "responsibility system," to family contracts that linked individual effort to immediate returns and provided every worker with a strong incentive to produce. The resutls seemed to confirm the theory but county leaders dealt only in passing or not at all with the many factors unrelated to material incentive that had also made impressive production records possible.

The most important objective factor undergirding rising yields is the water conservancy infrastructure—dams, irrigation works, river dykes—created by the collective labor of the past. Peasants built much of this infrastructure during the Great Leap, a movement derided by proponents of the "responsibility system" as ultra-left, voluntarist, and adventurist, but without that Leap how much water would there be to distribute in Fengyang today? Long before the Great Leap millions also worked to remold the Huai River basin. They built reservoirs to store run-off water and dykes to control what the reservoirs could not retain. Without this massive effort could anyone now hope to control floods on the lowlands along the treacherous Huai?

Other great engineering works will be necessary if Fengyang farmers hope to break through to new levels of crop production in the future. But can such works be carried out within the framework of the "responsibility system"? Can funds be raised to pay people to do individually for cash what they once did collectively for work points? In the past people invested their labor on projects that promised future benefit. They reaped the returns months or even years later. Now peasants demand payment by the day or by the month. Where will the necessary funds come from?

It came as no surprise to hear that labor supply presented no problem. I have already described how thousands of people now idle their way through the winter months waiting for spring planting time to come around again. Collectives once put their idle labor to work as a matter of course, a routine that wasted labor, so the charge goes, because peasant morale was so low. But did that waste really surpass the waste represented by the unused labor power of today?

Deputy County Chairman Wang assured me that huge projects are still possible. During the high water season of 1982 when the Huai River threatened to flood its banks, county leaders sent 30,000 people to work raising and strengthening the dykes. The county paid out no money but instead assigned every family, every individual, a quota to fulfill. Each individual who fulfilled his or her quota was free to go home. The work went fast and well, Wang said, much better than the collective work of the past.

This dyke work seemed to me, however, to be a special case. The Huai River in flood presents a clear and present danger to all inhabitants within its reach. County officials can mobilize people without pay to protect themselves from the river's backlash. But can they mobilize these same people without pay to build something useful to the future? And if they can do so will others not denounce the project as a revived form of leveling, another way to "eat out of one big pot"?

A second major factor undergirding Fengyang's rising yields is a national grain pricing system that generously rewards anyone who sells more grain to the state than his or her annual quota calls for. One or another variant of this system has been in effect for a long time. It is not something initiated by the post-gang of four leadership, as some recent reporting implies. As the system works today, above-quota grain sells at prices 50 percent higher than the national standard. Because Fengyang peasants produced so little in the past their quotas had always been low. As soon as they managed to push yields up they began to harvest above-quota grain and to sell it at premium prices. Premium prices swelled incomes and enabled the peasants to invest more in production, which in turn pushed yields still higher. As yields continued to rise the amount of grain sold at premium prices soon outweighed the amount sold at standard prices. The extra income served to further accelerate the upward spiral. Today more than 80 percent of the grain produced in Fengyang county is above-quota grain and sells at 50 percent above the standard price. This means that China as a whole is subsidizing agricultural investment and crop production in Fengyang. Wealth is flowing in at an unprecedented rate, a rate that cannot be sustained over the countryside as a whole. The "responsibility system" set this process in motion by unleashing peasant initiative, but once the process started extra profits derived from selling grain above its normal price added a whole new dimension to the local economy. As funds poured in people invested many of them in draft power and supplies for increased crop production and reaped benefits that went way beyond the added increment of human labor expanded. Attributing all progress to the "responsibility system" obscures the impact of the high prices for above-quota grain that fueled so much of that progress.

Money without supplies, of course, could not accomplish anything. A third major factor contributing to higher yields since 1978 has been the rising level of technical and material support—support that did not exist or existed only in embryo in the 1960s. When I asked the peasants for specific reasons why their yields went up they all said "the incentive to work provided by the contract." But when I countered with the suggestion that hard work alone could hardly quadruple yields on any piece of land they all said, "Of course, we bought more fertilizer."

It turned out that they are now not only buying and applying four to five times as much fertilizer per acre as before but they are also applying phosphorus along with nitrogen for the first time (potash they still neglect). More fertilizers coupled with more complete fertilizers have had a startling effect on yields. When I asked why they had not bought more fertilizer in the past they said they had always been too poor. But surely the state had long been prepared to loan money for the purchase of plant food. I suspect that ten years ago no adequate supplies existed. If cooperating peasants had somehow found money for fertilizers in the past they could not have exchanged it for such an abundance of materials in any case.

When I asked if there were any other good reasons for rising yields the peasants all said "good seed." They praised several varieties of winter wheat but spoke most enthusiastically about that truly significant breakthrough—hybrid rice. Hybrid rice, which has just about doubled the yields obtained throughout the county, was not available five years ago. The "responsibility system" came along just in time to seize this new technology and put it to work. The technology in turn helped make the "system" look good. Can one say that the old-style cooperatives could not have used hybrid rice to advantage? I think not. The history of the introduction of hybrid corn in Shanxi many years ago indicates the opposite.

Pursuing the topic of the material base for high yields, the peasants also cited timely pest control. Every family, it seems, now owns a packsack sprayer for applying insecticides and fungicides to rice, wheat, beans, and tobacco. When problem insects or fungi show up the people go out and annihilate them within a few hours. In the past whole teams had only one or two sprayers. When I asked, "Why so few?" the people replied: "We couldn't afford more. We were too poor."

Perhaps the "responsibility system" is the catalyst that makes all contributing factors productive. Perhaps without it the villages of Fengyang would continue to stagnate. It must be remembered, however, that Fengyang production started at such an abysmally low level that it could only go up. After four years the peasants are only now reaching levels of crop and sideline production that many other counties in China reached long ago through collective effort. The real test of the new system will come when local peasants try to push beyond such levels to heights as yet unscaled in Fengyang or elsewhere. Playing catchup ball, bringing into play all the material factors that have matured in China in the last two decades, is relatively easy. Breaking through to new levels of achievement will be much harder.

At the provincial capital of Hefei commune leaders told us that they were beginning to bump up against the upper limits of the production they considered possible on the land. To maintain momentum and guarantee further rises in living standards they looked to specialization, much of it involving livestock—poultry keeping, dairying, cattle feeding, pig raising, rabbit raising, bee keeping—and to nonfarm sidelines such as the large hotel that one brigade had already begun to operate. Almost every specialty the officials mentioned required intensive manual labor, as did every form of crop culture they talked of promoting. None of them seemed to be thinking in terms of raising the productivity of labor on the land through mechanization. Yet this is probably the most important way to guarantee not only rising living standards but further gains in per-unit yields.

That Chinese provincial and regional leaders now downgrade mechanization is hardly accidental. Even though years ago collectivization created a material base for tractor farming; even though recognizing this Mao put mechanization high on the agenda as early as 1958, very few functionaries at any level ever paid serious attention to it. Now that the "responsibility system" has broken up the material base by fracturing the land into countless small strips it is very difficult for anyone to take machinery seriously. Carving up the land has destroyed all economies of scale and has rendered meaningful mechanization all but impossible.

"Our land is foothill land," said Deputy County Chairman Wang as we drove through a wide, flat plain that ended finally against the dykes of the Huai River. "If we use machines at all they must be small, multipurpose machines adapted to hillside fields," he added. Yet on that day, throughout the day before, and on the day after, we drove through one spacious flat after another before arriving at rolling land that was almost as well suited to mechanization as the plain from which it emerged.

Defying logic, Wang continued to talk about foothills and small machinery, as if mechanization must start at and be tailored to the most forbidding terrain in the county instead of the most favorable. By concentrating on the difficulty of mechanizing the broken land at the fringes of his domain Wang avoided coming to grips with the adverse geographic consequences of the "responsibility system," with the disruptive effect of contracts on the size of fields on flat land. Mechanization had to fit the whole county, he seemed to be saying, or fit none of it. Thus it did not matter if the new policy destroyed the main factor favorable to machine agriculture, the wide sweep of the collective fields over most of the county in the past.

Wang predicted that as the peasants prospered they would buy machinery, form small groups for joint tillage, and put together plots of land large enough to make mechanization meaningful. Such a development may occur, but the natural obstacles are formidable. It took the momentum of a tremendous mass movement backed by the entire party to unify the land 25 years ago. Now that it has once again been broken up into millions of fragments so that each family can contract an equal per capita share, can those families stitch more than a fraction of it back together again?

If they cannot, what hope is there for raising labor productivity on the land? Clearly the "responsibility system" in Fengyang has unleashed some significant productive forces, but it has also thrown up some formidable material barriers to their long-range development. It is difficult to see how the peasants, now competing rather than cooperating as family units, will overcome these barriers.

New theories defining agriculture as a uniquely individualistic occupation have added ideological barriers to any future joint tillage, barriers that may prove to be as formidable as the material ones. County leaders have now concluded that farming is inherently unsuited to collective action and centralized direction. Because the process of crop and livestock production takes months to run its course, because along the way unforeseen variables inevitably force split-second changes in course, because changes in course require the immediate and thorough implementation of remedial measures, the process demands a high degree of flexibility, independence, and self-motivation. Only the most direct link between the process and the producer will do. Any dilution of that link, any deferral of responsibility, will lead to apathetic, business-as-usual, wait-until-tomorrow attitudes that invite disaster.

According to this new general theory only dispersed family management satisfies the requirements set by nature for production in the countryside. Wang Yongxi, Fengyang's second secretary, presented the idea as if it expressed an economic law, a law like that of supply and demand. "After trying so many things over so many years and failing so badly with a variety of collective arrangements, we are forced to conclude that centrally led cooperation in agriculture stands in contradiction to the very essence of the process it attempts to promote. There is something about the cycle of production in farming from planting to cultivating to harvesting that is incompatible with central direction and mass participation. All our failures in the past stem from one primary failure, our failure to recognize this principle."

Wang's extraordinary conclusion overthrows completely all those earlier maxims around which the Communist Party organized collective agriculture to begin with. In 1956 Liao Luyen summed them up:

"Cooperative farming, by pooling land, wipes out borders and unnecessary paths between fields and so brings more land under cultivation (5 percent more on the average).

"Cooperative farming makes it possible to carry out water conservancy projects, water and soil conservation, and land and soil improvement on a large scale. Cooperative farming makes it possible to transform arid land into irrigated fields, and barren and waste land into fertile soil.

"Cooperative farming makes it possible to use the full abilities of all men and women, those who are able-bodied, and those who are not fully able-bodied, and those who can do light tasks, enabling them all to engage in many fields of work to help develop production in agriculture, forestry, cattle breeding, subsidiary occupations, and fishing.

"Cooperative farming makes it possible to have single management of the farm, to cultivate crops best suited to the various types of soil, to put more labor power into improving the land, to improve cultivation by deep plowing and careful weeding, better techniques of sowing and planting; to improve the organization of field work; to improve the yields per mou."

The rejection of the above propositions may sound like total repudiation for cooperative agriculture, like a platform for return to the traditional desperate go-it-alone peasant tillage of the past. The advocates of the "responsibility system" deny it. They see the new system as socialist in form, a system that gives individual initiative a chance to develop inside a collective framework. This framework includes public (state) ownership of the main means of production, the land, which cannot be bought, sold, rented out, or rented in. It also includes a collective support network, the peasant-owned supply and marketing cooperatives that with backing from the state deliver all critical supplies and market most if not all the commodities produced. The macrosystem, the innovators say, is collective. Within it, at a microlevel, the peasants plan, invest, and labor individually because agricultural production demands personal attention to every detail. This, so the argument runs, is socialism tailored to China's unique rural situation.

Without getting into a debate over whether the system qualifies as socialist or not, one can grant that it is working reasonably well and quite fairly in Fengyang after four years, but one can also foresee that the dynamic individualism unleashed by family contracts may rise to challenge and eventually overthrow the collective integument that now supports and contains it. Many long-range questions remain unanswered.

From the social point of view the main question is that of polarization. One of the primary arguments in favor of collectivization when it was launched in the 1950s was that it would forestall social differentiation, block the break-up of rural society into exploiting and exploited classes. The peasants, so the cooperators argued, would all rise together. In practice collectivization did forestall polarization, but in too many cases no significant rise occurred. All remained poor together, eating out of one pot that wasn't anywhere near big enough and, worst of all, wasn't growing.

Reacting to this deplorable state of affairs, advocates of the "responsibility system" now boldly advocate the idea that "some must get rich first." Such a principle obviously favors the young, the strong, the healthy, the smart, and the aggressive. I asked what measures could prevent a handful of ambitious peasants on the rise from taking possession of the best means of production other than land—draft animals, carts, tractors, pumps, threshing machinery—and using these to exploit their less fortunate neighbors. In the lower stage coops of the 1950s a peasant with two animals could live without working. Could not a peasant with several tractors do so today? And if the tractors were passed on to the next generation would not the family perpetuate its privileged class position?

Deputy County Chairman Wang did not see this as a serious issue. In the past, he said, there were 27,000 needy families in the county, some 30 percent of the total. (He defined "needy" as families with less than 700 catties of grain per capita per year and less than 50 yuan per capita cash income.) Now, he said, there are only 1,021 such families in the whole county and the government gives them ten different kinds of special aid designed to keep them from sinking. The aid is as follows:

(1) Each state and local cadre takes personal responsibility for one needy family; studies its situation, and gives advice.

(2) Needy families pay no taxes.

(3) The county sets aside 50,000 yuan to help the needy buy fertilizer, chemicals, improved seeds, and other necessities.

(4) The county allocates 30,000 yuan for low-interest production loans to the needy, setting the interest rate at 1 percent instead of the 4.8 percent charged by the bank.

(5) Communes and brigades allocate an additional 30,000 yuan for similar production loans.

(6) Schools collect no fees from needy scholars.

(7) Needy families have the right to buy animal feed at reduced prices and to sell their grain to the state at any time, even when the State Grain Company, due to local oversupply, stops buying from the public.

(8) Needy families pay no doctors' fees (they still pay for medicine).

(9) The supply coop guarantees all necessary fertilizer to the needy. Others have to buy fertilizer where they can find it.

(10) Livestock specialists give needy families free help and waive fees for breeding services, the sterilization of young pigs, etc.

Wang said senior citizens without descendants also received special help:

"We give each one 700 catties of per capita grain, 6 catties of vegetable oil, a ton of grass, straw, and stalks for fuel, 30 yuan for clothes, 30 yuan for medical care, and 40 yuan for spending money. This amounts to 300 yuan of aid each year and with this aid the senior citizens can take care of themselves."

"One of the motives behind such aid," he added, "is to strengthen the birth control campaign. When young people see that old folks without descendants can survive they feel less pressure to have children and especially the sons who will support them in their old age."

To illustrate local policy toward needy families Wang took us to see Chen Defang, a widow with four children who was farming 17 mou (almost 3 acres) of land. She owned five sections of new housing, complete with some good furniture, shared a water buffalo with a neighbor, and was raising two pigs that she estimated would be worth 200 yuan apiece when grown. With help from her brother, her sister, and her sister-in-law (her own seventeen-year-old son was away at school) she had raised 133 bushels of wheat and rice (an average yield of 47 bushels per acre) and had sold half of it to the state (80 percent of this at premium prices). Although her income far surpassed the standards set for the needy she got special aid from the county, the brigade, and the team because her husband had been killed in the brigade stone quarry while doing collective work. She paid no taxes, no fees for education for her children, and no fees for medical care (medicines excepted). The county supplied her with a ton of mixed fertilizer, most of it free, while the brigade gave her 180 yuan, and the team 72 yuan, to defray production expenses. The county also gave her a "needy family" book that entitled her among other things to sell grain to the state at any time. Looking closely at this book Deputy County Chairman Wang began to scratch his head. She had sold much more grain than she had harvested. Most of this grain belonged to neighbors who had borrowed her book so they could sell their grain with ease. They had presumably paid her something for the privilege. Embarrassed by exposure, Widow Chen assured Wang that she would not abuse her book in the future.

What Deputy County Chairman Wang described and demonstrated to us was a sort of safety net for the disadvantaged. It was financed primarily by the taxes and cash contributions made to local brigades, communes, and county governments by all member families as part of the obligation they undertook with their land contracts. Yet it seemed that by itself, such a safety net could hardly prevent polarization or forestall exploitation. One of Widow Chen's neighbors already owned two tractors. Hauling freight on the road each tractor could earn 2.8 yuan per ton kilometer and gross something like 1,000 yuan a month. These 15-horsepower, 4-wheeled diesels, with small 2-ton wheeled trailers to match, cost 4,900 yuan per set. Any peasant could buy one and pay for it in full with hauling fees in less than six months. During the planting and harvest seasons a tractor-owning peasant could also do custom work for his neighbors—plowing at 1–1.5 yuan per mou and threshing at 2 yuan per hour. With diesel oil at .30 yuan per catty and consumption at 1–2 catties per hour net income could be high. Did this net income figure, I asked, include some rip-off of the neighbors' wealth?

Wang denied any such possibility. He saw these earnings as a legitimate return on the capital invested, as a reimbursement for legitimate operating expenses and as payment for the skilled labor expended. He defined exploitation as unearned income derived from speculation (playing the market), loans at usurious rates, or any attempt to revive the land rents of old. Payments by peasants to each other for services performed did not, by definition, involve exploitation. Wang based this conclusion on a theory widely held and propagated in China today concerning land ownership. In Chinese agriculture, the argument runs, the principal means of production is land. Exploitation has arisen historically based on the private ownership of land. Since the land is now held in common and no one can gain the use of more than a fair per capita share, no material base for exploitation exists and no such problem can arise in the future.

Given the history of the rise of capitalism this is an ingenuous theory, to say the least. Under capitalism the primary means of production has never been land, but machinery, plant, and industrial capital. By controlling such resources entrepreneurs have been able to profit from wage labor. Private ownership of the land hinders rather than advances this ability, forcing entrepreneurs to share their profits with a non-productive class of landowners. Numerous economists, from Karl Marx to Henry George, have argued that nationalization of the land would create ideal conditions for capitalist development. Various bourgeois revolutionaries have also advocated this, but historically the capitalists as a class have always made compromises with their landholding opposition to secure cooperation against the even more radical demands of the newly formed working classes.

What after all is Wang's "legitimate return on the capital invested" by the tractor owner? Is it not income channeled to him as the owner of a vital means of production which the recipient of the service must pay for at rates that reflect the going rate of profit? When the owner of the tractor is also its driver the exploitative element in the relationship may be obscured but it exists nevertheless. If the owner of the tractor hired someone to drive it a second form of value skimming would be added—the exploitation of wage labor.

One can agree with Deputy County Chairman Wang that payments to a few individuals for the services they render with privately owned machines is not very threatening. One can even argue that promoting private ownership of small means of production of this type and guaranteeing the profits that accrue to their owner-operators is essential to the development of China's economy today. But it borders on obscurantism to deny the exploitative potential of privately owned machinery while concentrating all fire on private land ownership as the source of class differentiation.

Newly developing trade channels can also open the road to exploitation and polarization. The biggest individual incomes in Fengyang now derive, as might be expected, not from agricultural production but from money made buying and selling commodities on the open market. Wang told us of one man in particular who was channeling thousands of yuan into his pocket selling the mats we saw woven by the lake to buyers in the Northeast. This trader paid as high as 3.2 yuan per mat (the official price was 2 yuan) and sold them a thousand miles away for considerably more, making in a season as much as 20,000 yuan profit. Officially he was just another individual who had a contract with the commune—this one authorized him to handle its trade in mats. He paid 10,000 yuan annually for the contract and in return received a letter of introduction from the commune and drafts from the local bank to finance purchases and transportation costs. Because he made 20,000 yuan above all costs, the state taxed him heavily, demanding as much as 15,000 as its share. This still left him 5,000 yuan in a county where the average per capita income was 345. He could plow this money back into his own business, put it in the bank to draw interest, or buy shares in some of the new industries under construction. Whatever he did with it, the income derived from the investment must be classified as unearned and must eventually accumulate as a substantial capital holding. How long could this man be called a mere peddler? Surely the commercial freedom that now pervades the market threatens to throw up some merchant princes.

The new industries we saw at Gaojen commune also seemed to open paths to serious differential enrichment. Buying a share brought with it the right to work in the new flour mill, but how long will mill workers remain the principal shareholders? Suppose the original shareholding worker retires, and suppose the heir has no interest in the mill but inherits the original owner's share and vote. Does the new owner not become an absentee owner, a coupon clipper drawing income from the neighbors' labor? One can foresee a process of differentiation here that with the passage of time may generate a class of owners who profit from the mill and a class of workers who operate it. Investing a share seems to be generating productive forces at an accelerating rate, but it is also opening the road to living without working.

Polarization may be the most disturbing negative threat posed by the "responsibility system," but it is by no means the only serious one. The system has led to severe disrupton of the birth control campaign, declining school attendance, flagrant misuse of land, and indiscriminate felling of trees. It has also led in many areas to the open robbing of ripe crops, right out of the fields. Families with land under contract need children to help with the farm work. They circumvent regulations to give birth to more children than the state allows and as their children grow they often keep them out of school to supplement adult labor. Many families build houses without permission on the land they have contracted, while others bury dead relatives in the middle of the best plots, reducing the tilled area. Family members also open sloping wasteland that should never be tilled and they cut trees along the public highways and canals at night for building material and for furniture making.

When I asked Wang about these problems he did not deny that they existed but treated them as temporary aberrations that can and will be brought under control. He said that the birth rate had risen sharply after the land was divided, but with incomes rising and a stepped-up campaign for family planning now organized from above, it was slowing down again. He said that school attendance had dropped from 95 percent to 88 percent but had now jumped back to 90 percent. As the peasants became more prosperous they began to think once more about the importance of education for their children. He said that many people had built houses illegally on contracted land but that county authorities had stepped in and stopped the practice. He pointed out a pile of building stone in an open field, obviously in preparation for some new construction, but said that the owner had already been warned that he could not build there and had agreed to remove the stones. As for graves on productive land, we saw far too many of them, both old and new. Wang made no claim to having solved this problem but said that the practice was illegal. We also saw many stumps of freshly cut trees beside the highway and long stretches that contained no trees at all, though trees had been planted in the past. Wang said that to combat this form of vandalism the county was parceling out the highway embankments to individual families as part of the "responsibility system" and predicted that the trees would survive better in the future. We saw very little hill land and so could not estimate how much of it the peasants were rashly opening up to uncontrolled erosion. As for the robbing of crops, all Fengyang leaders and peasants to whom we talked flatly denied that it was a problem. "Who would want to take grain these days?" they asked. "We all have more grain than we can sell. We stack it up in the street outside our houses, and no one takes it. No, robbing grain is not a problem here." I assume that they spoke the truth but I could not understand why the open robbing so endemic in Shanxi ever since family contracting began had never plagued Fengyang. Perhaps the enthusiasm and thoroughness of the county leadership had established a different climate for law and order there.

Is Wang right about the future? Can the many problems outlined above be brought under control as he insists, or are they contradictions built into a new system that proudly proclaims "a few must get rich first"? I find it hard to judge such a question at this time. Observing Fengyang the problems appeared minor in contrast to the accomplishments, but in other areas this relationship appeared to be reversed. What seemed to make the least sense was forcing everyone to break up collective work on the land. Why not preserve those cooperatives that have been successful and let them compete with contracting individuals? Why not make room for some variety in social organization and see which system produces the best results in the long run? One may make such a plea, but in China it seems the wind of policy can only blow from one direction at a time and the knife of implementation has to cut a clean slice all the way to the bottom of the pile. In the Middle Kingdom pluralism has no precedent.

大回潮 Reform in Stride: Rural Change 1984

After the initial land reform in China, the agrarian system developed into two-tiered cooperatives. By 1958 and the Great Leap Forward, these cooperatives amalgamated into a third tier of much larger units, which became known as the People's Communes. With certain modifications and policy shifts, these communes remained at the core of rural organization until 1980, when their dismantlement began. Now, most peasant families contract land from local authorities in an arrangement known as the responsibility system.

To understand the impact of this new system on Chinese agriculture, you have to have a picture of China's countryside. While in the West it is common for farmers to live on farms and work the land around, in China, especially in the north, people instead live in very crowded villages and go out to the fields beyond. When you fly over the North China Plain, you see villages scattered all over, not more than a mile apart, often closer, and each with 1,000 to 3,000 people. These villages are growing while the open land is shrinking, so that you have an increasingly concentrated rural population trying to survive on dwindling land resources. There is less tillable land in China than there was in 1949, but the population has almost doubled.

The responsibility system is in some ways a revival of the policy called *san zi yi bao* (roughly, three freedoms—one contract), instituted in 1962 after the debacle of the Great Leap Forward. The three

This article is a shortened version of a talk given in London in 1984 and printed in *China Now*, no. 113, Summer 1985.

74

freedoms were freedom to enlarge the area of private plots, to expand free markets, and to foster small profit-making enterprises, and the one contract was the contract made by each individual family for set quotas of grain to be delivered at state prices.

Throwback to the 1960s?

This system spread very widely in the early 1960s and offers some interesting parallels with today. Of course, freedom to expand private plots pales into insignificance when almost the whole of the land is contracted privately as now. The expansion of markets and the setting up of individual sidelines for profit are the most important adjuncts to the whole policy, but the heart of it remains contracting out the land family by family.

When the contracts first started, they were temporary and indefinite in term. Later the term was set at three years. Now contracts are for fifteen years, with inheritance rights. If the contractor dies within fifteen years, descendants can inherit the contract and carry it through. This is all but universal in China now. Complications arise because there are many forms of contract. In Anhui, which is where it all began, they are very simple: the peasant contractor pays a certain cash amount which goes to local government, sells a certain agreed amount of grain to the state at state prices, pays some basic taxes, and keeps everything else. There is no percentage of the harvest to hand over, so there is no variable in this system, just a certain fixed sum which the higher authorities must have.

Other forms are more complicated, often entailing an obligation to turn over grain to the local village office. This grain earns work points, and the contractor gets back a share, with cash distribution once or twice a year. In yet another form, only part of the land is contracted. The community reserves the rest and each peasant agrees to work so many days on this public land. There are also variations where groups can contract. And sometimes the amount contracted is determined by the number in the family, sometimes by the number of ablebodied workers in a family. Most variations revolve around contracting resources out to the family as a production unit.

The big advantage of contracting from the point of view of the authorities is that it automatically solves the question of reward according to work performed. Each family works on its own resources, and whatever the members raise reflects the work they have put in. The system does not need much planning; it does not take much organizing; it does not take much leadership. There are no accounts to keep, not a lot of meetings to be held—each family takes care of itself. Also, no one is responsible for poor results except the contractor. The authorities simply give the resources to the individuals and tell them to enrich themselves, and if in five years they are not rich it is their own fault. Certainly no one can blame the authorities.

Fostering Specialization

Contracting goes along with a wide-open market, which is very important. For instance, a contractor may have a contract to deliver a certain amount of grain, but he does not have to raise that grain himself: he can raise cotton or other crops, whatever he thinks is more profitable, and can buy the grain from somebody else and deliver that to the government to meet the grain quota. That has become quite common in some places, to the point where grain production has dropped off sharply and new regulations have to be established requiring people to raise the grain they owe.

The market has stimulated all sorts of small sidelines. Under the commune system, where it was badly led, handicrafts were often discouraged and special products were also discouraged. People did not feel free to go to market. With no outlet for the things they made, they just stopped making them. Now with a wide-open market people can start making whatever they want and generally find an outlet for it. So people are specializing in all sorts of things, even strange ones: one peasant is raising scorpions, for example. A lot of people have gone into beekeeping. China is a land of great variety, multiple resources, and remarkable ingenuity and although I do not think that the cooperative system by necessity suppressed this ingenuity—in many cases it promoted it—certainly the new policy has unleashed a great deal of individual creativity.

Along with the free market goes the freedom to set up individual or cooperative enterprises for profit. Shareholding industrial cooperatives are much in order today, and many people are pooling capital and setting up enterprises that resemble joint stock companies. Along with this goes the right to hire and fire people. At first the government set limits on the number of employees permitted in a private enterprise. For a while it was said you could hire six or eight people; then you could hire as many people as you wanted as long as they were family members—not a very stringent restriction since in many Chinese communities everyone has the same surname and could be called a relative. Now even those restrictions have gone out the window and hiring is essentially unlimited.

The tremendous increase in marketing has provided an income for large numbers of people as peddlers and sellers as well. You see things you have not seen for twenty years in China: grown men sitting in front of three apples or four pears trying to sell them on the street. You didn't find ablebodied people doing that kind of task in China five years ago. For a time there were efforts to regulate peddling and various definitions of what constituted peddling as distinct from profiteering. One definition specified that as many goods as can be loaded on a bicycle was peddling and not profiteering, while taking the goods by train or truck would be speculation. Now, anything goes.

Finally, people now have the right to buy and own productive equipment privately, like tractors or machinery, trucks, processing equipment, and so on. Such ownership is now very widespread.

Probably 98 percent of all the land in China has been contracted out and that even applies to a large sector of state farms. State farms were set up to demonstrate modern production or simply to reclaim waste land. In Northeast China they were part of a major effort to establish a grain based in the virgin lands. Many state farms no longer operate as a single management unit: their resources are simply rented to the staff, who raise whatever they like and pay rent, called a "contract price," and the rent collected shows as profit to the farm.

Economic Results

While I do not think grain production has increased as much in the last few years as has been claimed, clearly grain is not in short supply. The price of free market grain is dropping and approaching that of state grain, which would not happen if there was any major shortage. Furthermore, some people are feeding a great deal of livestock—12,000 hens or 125 pigs per family—something they could not do if grain were not available. The situation is particularly good with coarse grains such as maize, sorghum, and so on, which people do not like to eat. In the past most people had to eat these, but now they eat wheat and rice and feed more coarse grains to livestock.

But in some places there has actually been a big decline in grain production; people have shifted to other things or even abandoned land. In parts of Hunan, for instance, they just left the land and went off to find some other work.

At the same time, "economic crops" have really shot up; cotton production has doubled, and oil seeds and other special crops such as fruit and vegetables have shown significant increase. Yields in China, which good cooperatives once got and which outstanding individuals now get are close to world yield levels, as high as the best farmers in Europe and America. So there will not be some quick way to double this and double it again.

But while these good results are quite well publicized, other consequences are less well known. One of these is the fragmentation of the land, which is quite extraordinary. One of the most promising things in the collective system in terms of future modernization was the fact that the land had been put together in a very practical way. Fields were large; machines, if they had them, could have gone to work easily in China, as there was the physical base for modernization. Now that base no longer exists. The land is much more fragmented than it was before land reform.

One reason for this of course is that there are twice as many families on the land. Another reason is that officials tried to do the contracting fairly. This meant that almost every family in the village got a piece of each quality of land. Every family also got a strip of the near field, and a strip of the far field, so that each big piece was cut into hundreds of small strips. Since the original fields were big, and access is necessary to each small strip, they gave each family a piece stretching from one road to the next, which means a long and narrow strip. The same area might be reasonable if it were shaped as a square, but all these strips cause great difficulties. Many are so narrow that even a cart can't go

down them, which means that everything has to be carried in and out
on a carrying pole. Also, there are endless quarrels about strip widths
and cheating: "I robbed a furrow from you and you robbed a furrow
from me." The courts are loaded with lawsuits concerning land use and
irrigation rights and so on.

Fragmentation has not affected yields that much yet, because peasants are still farming with hoes, after all, and it really doesn't matter
with hoe agriculture whether the strip is a yard wide or 10 acres in one
bloc—except that it involves much more labor. Peasants are just working harder, working more hours, putting in more effort; there is a
general speedup in agriculture and this extraordinary effort is maintaining yields or even raising them.

Destruction of Resources

The long-term destruction of resources that belong to the collective
is one of the worst results of the new system. In many cases, collective
assets were simply broken up and sold to individual bidders; when it
became clear that the collective's property was going to be contracted
out, people came and dismantled whatever belonged to them jointly,
including the headquarters, school, any publicly owned machinery,
and so on. They took window frames out, doors off, and the beams out
of the roof. In Horse Square commune, near Long Bow, there was a big
public piggery. We photographed what remained of it after it was
dismantled. It was no great structure to start with and no one of course
got rich raiding a few beams from it but it was quite a mess when they
got through. When Long Bow had to join the system, the leaders met
in secret and put the militia on guard so that the entire property of the
collective would not be dismantled while they were meeting to decide
what to do. In that case they avoided destruction.

Destruction has also increased sharply in terms of the environment.
Trees have been cut down in great numbers, and around Beijing, even
telephone poles and powerlines have been cut down, for the wood,
because of the great furniture market that exists in the city. And in the
mountains north of Beijing land of all kinds has been opened up;
people opened up land on 45-degree slopes.

I've traveled on the same train north from Beijing for four summers, and I never saw the mountains opened up as they are now. The slopes might have been overgrazed, but at least they were not tilled. If they were covered with brush there might have been a small amount of firewood cut there, but now there are huge areas being opened and tilled with a hoe and planted to crops. This can perhaps be done for two or three years and then the slopes will be finished. The soil on those slopes is in great danger. Other cropped areas that should never be plowed will be destroyed by wind erosion. Houses are rising up and graves are appearing in the middle of good crop land. People are burying their dead in the fields as they did in the old days; they are burying people in the land that they contract as if it were their own.

When you raise questions about these ravages people tell you it is a matter of controlling abuses, resolving them with new laws and alert police action. But some of these people are getting so prosperous they will be able to defy the laws and pay off the police.

Hired Hands Make It Work

The whole thrust of the new policy is supposed to enable the socialist principle of distribution, "to each according to his work," to be realized. But since each family can contract more capital goods, and even more land than they can operate themselves, they can hire others to do the work. People told me proudly of a man in northern Shanxi who had contracted 750 mu (well over 100 acres). I said he must have a lot of machinery, but they said no, he doesn't have any machinery, he hires the labor. And in a brigade north of Taiyuan 80 mu (12 acres) of rice land had been contracted by one couple, along with almost 10 acres of other crop land, again hiring people to work the land.

The size of some of the new private enterprises is constantly growing. The paper showed a picture of the first peasant in China to buy a car, a woman. Her enterprise is egg production, and she is raising chickens and marketing eggs on her own. From the figures it is quite clear she has at least 12,000 hens, and her family cannot supply enough labor power to raise that many hens. I would estimate she has ten or fifteen people working in that enterprise, so she is hiring quite a few.

Another peasant mentioned in the press was making sausage. He had four family members. But his sausage business grew so much that a few months ago he hired four skilled workers, each of whom brought an apprentice. By any definition of the past, if a family hires more labor than it contributes itself, it is a rich peasant family.

At the start, of course, the contractor maintains the old relationships. The wage equivalent of the work-points people used to earn is paid by the contractor, who takes a modest amount as his own salary. But no one has control over later developments. Long Bow had six gardens—each of them about six acres—with fifteen people sharing work and income. The gardens were contracted to the highest bidder and then each contractor hired fifteen people to do the work at well below standard wages.

In addition, there is an enormous growth in the number of middlemen or commission merchants. These people are in control of resources and handle transportation. For instance, there is a man who has responsibility for moving all the cement out of the cement mill in Long Bow and bringing in all the raw materials. He hires the carts that haul the goods. If the cart is local—that is to say, if it belongs to a village resident, he gets 10 percent of the earnings of each load. If it is not local, he gets 20 percent. A man like this is making big money.

The authorities claim that peasant income has now doubled—quite an achievement. But the figure may not have been corrected for inflation, because it is clear that this period has seen a sharp rise in prices as well—city people are complaining about food prices being much higher.

What is involved in all of this is not just income differentiation but class differentiation. Those who get rich first preempt the high ground and end up exploiting those who have lagged behind. There is also something troubling going on with regard to the so-called free market. In one case a gang took over a tomato market where peasants were bringing in fresh tomatoes, forcing the peasants to sell their produce behind a building and then selling directly to the people in the market themselves. I'm not sure how widespread such strongarm methods are, but they are ugly, and they are expanding.

Any system that disregards limits on the amount of resources that can be contracted does not end up distributing rewards based on work performed. What develops is a system that bases rewards on the amount of productive resources contracted. The capital controlled soon outweighs the work done.

Gruesome Customs

The new system also radically affects the quality of life: the more the system reflects the old economic relations or turns toward traditional economic relations, the more traditional culture and customs revive. This was brought home to us rather gruesomely in Long Bow by the death and burial of two old peasants last August. Ordinarily, people bury the dead as soon as possible, particularly in August! But now almost everyone that has a death in the family goes to the soothsayer or oracle in the village for a proper date for the burial. It is important not only where but when you bury a person, the stars have to be right. And this oracle turns out to be someone who was once sort of regarded as the village fool; they called him *ba mao*, which means "eight dimes" (since there are ten dimes in a dollar, eight means not all there). Somehow he inherited a book of oracles from his grandfather and he is now the chief seer of the village.

This fellow told the bereaved they should bury the body eight days after the person died. On the day of the burial—they don't bury the body till seven o'clock in the evening, about when the sun starts to go down—they display the coffin in different parts of the village and play music all day long. They hired a big band, and of course the bigger the band, the more prestige to the family; the more glory to the dead ancestor. This was really a sight because the corpse created such a stench that they could not play near it, so they had to leave it down the street about a hundred yards. As they played, some sort of gall was dripping from the coffin and making a puddle in the street and the flies were coming from all around. When they went to move the coffin after two hours of playing in one place they had to pour sorghum liquor all over the coffin to kill the odor and drive the flies off before they could get close enough to pick it up. It takes sixteen men to carry a coffin and they all had to get pretty close to it. Then they would move it down the street, set it in another place, and play for another two hours—another puddle of gall formed. This happened twice in the summer of 1983.

I also saw the revival of many traditional entertainments. There were

7 million people involved in amateur drama in China two or three years ago and now that is down to about 2.5 million. But there is a big rise in professional acts of all kinds, much of it rather low-level, like putting a snake in one nostril and bringing it out of the mouth, erotic dancing, and things like that. There is a real shift in the cultural output in rural areas.

More Labor Leaving Agriculture

One thing that interests me particularly is the enormous shift of labor out of agriculture that the new policy has brought about. I have long argued for mechanization, and over the years was always told, "We have too many people; how could we possibly do it?" And of course my view was that they should begin in places such as Long Bow which are suburban and where there is alternative employment for the released labor, and where the community is prosperous. Begin there, and work outward to solve the technical problems. It would progressively spread and maybe 20 percent would do it first and another 10 percent later, and then another 20 percent, and so on over many years. But no one ever listened to those arguments. And now the responsibility system has thrown about 30 percent of the people off the land in one year: the people who did not contract land. Of that 30 percent, only half have found anything else to do as of January 1984, so there is an enormous displacement based not on technical advance but simply on economic and social policy. No conceivable mechanization plan could have done that on that scale in that time. Say there are 300 million people engaged in farming in China. A third of that would be 100 million, and half of those unemployed—that is 50 million people. Where are they all? Of course, they are living off other family members or relatives or friends. They are not out looking for work, so this displacement is hidden.

All of this recalls some of the problems that emerged with the New Democracy program in China in the 1950s: the mixed economy was fostering capitalism in some sectors, generating polarization, displacement, and other problems. The solution in those days was to move toward collective agriculture. Now the government is reestablishing a mixed economy with a growing private sector. It is quite dynamic, and I think quite unstable. The question is: Which way will it go?

大回潮 The Situation in the Grasslands

Most expert observers agree that the grasslands, sandy lands, and deserts of China's northern tier are under extreme pressure and rapidly deteriorating. Pastures are turning into sand dunes, stable dunes are turning into roving dunes, and the roving dunes of the old desert areas are expanding south and east. Specialists estimate that the total yield of vegetative matter has been cut in half since 1950 while livestock numbers have quadrupled. The rising imbalance periodically leads to disasters such as the loss of 2,000,000 head in Xilinhote in 1977 and 10,000,000 head overall in 1984. Many officials, specialists and ordinary people pay much attention to these matters and debate both cause and cure.

In what follows I state some of my conclusions on the situation in the grasslands. They are based on five successive years of spring and fall experience in Wengnuite Banner working to build the Grasslands Demonstration Center there.

Focus on Overgrazing

The first question that needs to be settled is what is the source of the problem. What is the main reason for grassland deterioration and accelerated desertification? Clearly the problem is man made—the

This article is a revised version of an article that originally appeared in the *Inner Monogolian Journal of Social Science*, August 1985 lands are now under unbearable stress because they are over-grazed. They are overgrazed because they are overstocked. Too many head compete for too little vegetation on too few hectares of land.

Some people try to blame adverse climatic changes, the plowing up of virgin land, the search for medicinal herbs, damaging methods of hay making, an increase in grassland rodents, etc. for the trouble. I feel that these are all secondary factors. The climate may well be deteriorating because the range is deteriorating. Plowed land represents but the smallest fraction of the total area (less than three hundredths in Xilinhote). The same is true for dug herbs and poor hay making. We must not let the damage from these things divert our attention from the main problem—overgrazing. Once stock and resources have been brought into balance everything else will be easy to solve.

In order to deal with the main problem, overgrazing, several things must be done. First, concepts of stock raising must change. Herdsmen must come to see the range and its vegetation, and not their herds, as their major resource. Herds, in reality, amount to an input on the land, like the seed put in by a crop farmer.

Second, livestock numbers must be reduced to fit the carrying capacity of the range, and grazing must be well managed to preserve the energy the grass contains. Finally, the productivity of the range itself must be increased step by step.

The key measure is herd reduction. It is clear that something drastic must be done soon and on a large scale to cut livestock numbers. Thinking can and will change only gradually. Range improvement can only be slow. Moreover, it requires considerable investment. Herdsmen should grasp the key link now and that link is herd reduction.

In fact without herd reduction most range building measures will fail: hungry cattle and sheep break through fences, eat bark and leaves off trees, destroy new seedings, kill the brush on the dunes. But herd reduction cannot be a simple numbers game. Livestock numbers can be misleading, one cow can equal five to six sheep, one sheep can equal one and a half goats. If we reduce herds by killing off goats and horses (as has been done at Wengnuite) then replace some of them with sheep and cattle, total numbers may go down but feed requirements may well go up.

It is important to think not just of livestock numbers but of livestock units, taking a mature sheep as one, then rating everything in proportion to the feed requirements of different classes of stock. Most specialists do this, but many discussions and many reports do not take these differences into account.

The question often arises that if we reduce livestock numbers—that is, livestock units—will herdsmen be able to maintain their income and their living standards? The answer is that fewer livestock units do not necessarily mean lower incomes. In fact, if we fit livestock units to the resources of the range and manage them well we can increase both the quantity and the quality of the offtake (animals sold, animal products sold) and thus push incomes up, even doubling them in some cases.

Change the Management System

Good management requires little or no investment. It begins with the realization that the land is the main resource and that our goal should be to produce as much meat, wool, milk or other animal product per hectare as can be done without damage to vegetation, or still better, while improving vegetation. Good management means, primarily, keeping livestock unit numbers down to levels that the land can support. These numbers can vary depending on the composition of the herd—that is, the proportions between breeding females, replacements, and fattening animals—to minimize feed intake and maximize product offtake. The key thing here is to make every animal productive and move each off to market as soon as grown and ready, not carry them through nonproductive winters and extra seasons. With proper herd structure half the number of cattle can produce twice as much meat as is the general practice now. With proper flock structure a somewhat reduced flock of sheep can produce three times as much meat and 50 percent more wool than is now generally obtained. In addition, good management means carrying out wise grazing practices. Probably in the arid and semiarid regions of China's northern tier this means some sort of deferred grazing, rather than ordinary rotational grazing.

Another question concerns how one determines suitable herd/flock structure or composition. While much research needs to be done before this question can be concretely answered for any given location, the following example from Wengniute Ranch illustrates the general principles. In Table 1 current herd composition or structure is compared with a recommended or approved structure, taking as standard practice in the latter case the sale of fattened cattle at thirty months of age. These tables were worked out by the New Zealand expert Peter Harris.

Table 1. Actual and Potential Herd Composition

Animal	percent	Present regime	percent	Improved regime
Breeding cows	38	Energy cost per animal sold:	42	Energy cost per animal sold
Replacements	45	300–550 × 10(cubed) MJME	16	115–130 × 10(cubed) MJME
Beef/fattening	17	Selling rate: 4–8%	42	Selling rate: 29–31%

In the second table current flock structure is compared to a recommended structure:

Table 2. Actual and Potential Herd Composition

Stock	percent	Present regime	percent	Improved Regime
Sheep Wethers	26	Energy cost per animal sold	56	Energy cost per animal sold:
Replacements	30	58 × 10(cubed) MJME	16	18 × 10(cubed) MJME
Ewes	44	Energy cost per kg wool sold 1.4 × 10(cubed) MJME Selling rate 6%	28	Energy cost per kg wool sold: 1.0 × 10(cubed) MJME Selling rate 22%

Just by adjusting herd and flock structure and without increasing the feed base Wengniute Ranch could expect to increase annual sales of meat and wool as follows:

Table 3. Actual and Potential Sales of Meat and Wool

Total herd/ flock	Sales	Total herd/flock	Sales
Cattle 3225	140–270	1350–1405	385–485
Sheep 5320	325	4926	1084
	14,000 kg wool		20,200 kg wool

In practice, the increases illustrated might be somewhat less than the estimates but still the magnitude of the potential increases makes it very worthwhile to carry out the changes proposed.

Controlled experiments are also needed to determine the best grazing pattern to fit each local area. Generally, in arid and semiarid regions short-cycle rotational grazing doesn't work well because grass and legume recovery time is slow. Herdsmen prefer deferred grazing under such conditions. One method of deferred grazing is to set aside a large block of land (say one-third of the total) through spring and summer. Then after this block goes to seed graze it in the fall while the other two-thirds rest. The following year a different one-third of the land is set aside, thus allowing one-third of the land to rest and go to seed each year. Under such a regime the whole range will regenerate itself if it is not overgrazed. No seeding or other measures are necessary.

Since these measures make so much sense and cost so little to carry out (if the animals are herded not even fencing is needed—though fencing does help) one might reasonably ask why they haven't been widely used. There are three main reasons. First, in the past grass was plentiful, a resource as abundant as air or water. Wealth was measured only in terms of the number of livestock possessed. This led to the practice of chasing after animal numbers alone. Second, due to hard winters and probable mortality, herdsmen have traditionally tried to keep quite a few old steers on hand. Unlike pregnant cows and yearling calves, the steers were not under stress for growth or reproduction, hence they survived hunger and cold better. Though they lost in the winter and spring most of what they gained in the summer and fall, thus wasting large quantities of forage, they nevertheless provided security for the herdsmen and could be sold if necessary for emergency expenses—illness, marriage, funerals, and so on. Finally, the price system encouraged keeping older animals around. In the export market the heavier the steer the higher the price per kilogram. In all markets poor meat sold for the same price as quality meat so there was no advantage to selling young, well grown animals. In a period of price rises such as China went through recently, keeping animals on hand in anticipation of the next price rise certainly paid off.

For all these reasons most herdsmen still carry on in the traditional way maintaining herd/flock structures unsuited to the best use of resources and wasting enormous quantities of scarce forage. Under an improved regime, however, herdsmen can expect better survival rates. Insofar as animal unit numbers are reduced and the range improved, yearlings and breeding females could be expected to come through the winter in better shape than in the past, although special care still would have to be given to young and pregnant animals. Since herds would be smaller, stored forage such as hay and silage should last longer, thus reducing mortality. There is still an added risk, however, to such a regime. Perhaps the government could institute some form of stock insurance to provide security for those willing to take the new path.

Change the Pricing System

Perhaps the most important step the government could take to improve the situation on the grasslands would be a change in price policy. Changing price policy requires no investment, yet it could be a major factor in turning a bad situation around. Two suggestions: (a) all young cattle, such as first-year weaned calves sold as feeders, should command premium prices; and (b) well-grown fat cattle reaching good market weights at thirty months or under should command premium prices. Older animals, regardless of weight should sell as culls at reduced prices. There should be no rewards for extra weight unrelated to quality or to rapid growth such as now exist in the export market.

Such price changes would encourage people to sell off weaned calves as feeders or weaners for fattening elsewhere and would encourage others to sell young fat cattle before their third winter, thus maintaining an efficient herd structure. In 1984 many herdsmen told Mr Young (Australian livestock expert) that a price loading of 50 percent in favor of weaned calves would be enough to persuade them to sell their animals rather than keep them through the winter on poor feed. For sheep a bonus price for well grown fat lambs and for high fleece weights would accomplish the same thing.

A new price policy would be the most effective, most rational, and easiest thing for the government to put into effect under present circumstances. This would give a great boost to the livestock industry, help stop the destruction of the range, and lay the groundwork for a two-stage system of meat production, particularly beef production.

In the United States cattle ranchers in the arid and semiarid and mountainous regions practice a two stage system. They keep on hand only breeding cows, and raise weaned calves or yearling feeders for sale to feedlots in the grain surplus regions of their own or other states. The price structure rewards them for this with premium prices for young, well-grown feeder cattle. In the grain surplus regions the cattle are fed out and sold for beef at between eighteen and thirty months of age. Under such a system each zone concentrates on the production most suited to it and the zones complement each other. The range bears no pressure from fattening stock while the farming regions find an outlet for their grain. In Nebraska, the two stages of the system exist side by side. Ranchers raise cows and calves in the sandhills while farmers raise corn in the irrigated Platte River valley, then feed it out to feeders bought from the sandhills; surplus Nebraska feeders go to Iowa, Illinois, and even as far east as Pennsylvania.

With the aid of a good price structure it would be advantageous for China to move in this same direction. Young cattle from the arid and semiarid grasslands could go to river valleys where irrigation makes grain and silage stores possible, (for example, the irrigated flatlands along the lower Xilamulum River in Wengniute Banner). Grain surplus areas in Heilongjiang, Liaoning, Hopei, and perhaps Shanxi could set up feed lots. Such a disposal of livestock could take a lot of pressure off the grasslands and would be welcomed by the herdsmen if prices were right.

Alternative proposals stress not herd reduction but increasing the productivity of the range through measures such as seeded pastures, shelter belts, air seeding, increased use of fertilizers, widespread use of Kuluns (oases built around water sources), and larger acreages of crops for storage. As long as livestock numbers remain excessively high, however, any measures to increase range productivity will be extremely hard to carry out. Most measures such as seeding (whether by air or on the ground), dune fixation, tree planting, or crop enclosures depend on long-term exclusion of all stock if they are to work at all. The excluded livestock put excessive pressure on the remaining range, causing even more rapid deterioration than before. Recovery in one spot is paid for with blowouts and destruction elsewhere. In many cases herdsmen or livestock break through the fences, invade the excluded area, and take off whatever feed exists long before the plants have a chance to establish themselves.

Once unit numbers are brought into balance with resources and grazing is well managed, however, all these range-building measures can increase productivity and thus allow for reasonable increases in livestock unit numbers. Quite clearly range-building should be coordinated with balanced stocking rates and good grass management. If not it can easily be defeated. The ruins of many efforts can readily be seen when traveling through the grasslands.

Some Common Misconceptions

Some rational measures have often proven counterproductive. Increased winter feed supplies from irrigated land, for example, will not automatically lead to reduced stocking rates and less pressure on the land. In many cases, as soon as forage is stored in any form, herders simply increase the number of stock to the limit of the new feed supply and overload the range with even more head. New productive cropland should not be allowed to serve as an excuse to increase livestock numbers to the limit. The crops harvested should serve instead as supplements to the carrying capacity of the range and as emergency stores for hard winters, or as feedlot forage for fat cattle taken off the range and not carried through only to go back out to graze.

One common perception is that the range cannot be overloaded during the growing season, that harm is done by heavy grazing only before growth begins in the spring or after it ends in the fall. But this theory contradicts all scientific evidence. Plants can be badly damaged or even destroyed by close cropping during the growing season. They need time to store nutrients in the roots, they need to mature and set seed periodically. We cannot overgraze at will during, before, or after the growing season. Those who think otherwise do not have a very deep understanding of plant physiology.

Another common perception is that only after native stock have been upgraded can numbers be reduced without reducing income. This is a very questionable proposition. While improved breeds are often more productive than native breeds, under current levels of nutritional stress native breeds are performing well below their genetic potential. Bringing livestock numbers into balance with resources can sharply improve the performance of native breeds. This is just another way of saying that the limiting factor in livestock production now is not the genetic makeup of the animals but poor feeding levels, nutritional stress.

Under severe conditions of stress such as exist in the grasslands now improved breeds may often do worse than native breeds. High producing stock are not used to hardship and cannot survive cold and hunger as native breeds can. Today, first priority should be given to improving nutrition by cutting back numbers and adjusting herd and flock structure or composition. This will lay a firm foundation for breed improvement. This is not to say that all breed improvement efforts are useless now, but only to point out that what is most important is improving nutrition.

While the "responsibility system" has given many families the incentive they need to work hard and do well, at present, over much of the grasslands the worst possible combination holds sway—privately controlled stock grazing publicly owned lands. No one cares for the land because no one is responsible for it. Everyone tries to raise more animals and get as much as possible from the range, which is free to all. The result is an uncontrolled scramble for whatever forage exists out there and this amounts to a general attack on range vegetation. Contracting has accelerated the destruction of the range.

To overcome destruction, government officials are advocating contracting the range along with the stock to individual herdsmen. It is true that holding responsibility for the land should make the herdsmen much better caretakers than they are now. But I foresee many problems. In order to guarantee exclusive use most people will have to fence their range. This might work well on some flat lands and some gently rolling plains but it seems a solution unsuited to hilly or mountainous regions. The amount of range available per family is only 1,000 to 2,000 mou in most places, then up to 6,000 mou in others. Fencing off the range in squares or rectangles of that size will make rational use of resources difficult. Highlands should be grazed at different times from lowlands, and the same goes for range populated by different plant species. Situations such as exist at Wengniute Ranch where swamplands merge with rolling grazing lands that in turn merge into brush covered dunes require each family to have some land of each type, plus some near and some far dune land. It is hard to imagine a rational fencing scheme that will satisfy these varied demands.

On hill land, stock tend to run fence lines making paths that erode badly when pounded by rain. Fencing on the scale required must also be very expensive, not to mention the fact that it will completely change the character of the whole region, turning wide open grasslands into a fenced-in nightmare. Furthermore, it is not at all certain that individual families will manage their land well. Many a private owner has ruined a farm in the United States either out of ignorance or greed, or both. Can one expect Mongolian herdsmen to be so different?

Small voluntary joint herding groups would seem to offer a more practical way out. With eight, ten or more families herding together each fenced area could be 10,000, 20,000 or even 60,000 mou. This would make seasonal grazing within the fence possible and would cost much less per hectare or per head than fencing in individual family plots. Rangeland conditions seem to favor small scale cooperation over all out individual management.

Reduce Han Migration

One further problem remains: population increases leading to a demand for increased livestock numbers. If the population consisted only of the Mongolian minority this would not be a pressing problem. In the thirty-nine years since liberation the Mongolian population has gone up less than 50 percent. The total population of the region, however, has gone up by a factor of five. The great bulk of this represents Han Chinese in-migration and settlement, including the conversion of many Han migrants from tillers of land to herdsmen who run herds and flocks and compete for space on the overloaded range with the original Mongolian inhabitants. Many Mongolian Chinese feel that they could handle the range wisely if it were not for these vast in-migrations. There is some truth to this view and steps really should be taken to stop further Han settlement on the grasslands as herdsmen. There are many other opportunities for Han Chinese to make a contribution to the development of Inner Mongolia. It would make sense to push these opportunities and to discourage the further settling in of new herdsmen. The thrust behind this movement is the relatively high standard of living of many of the herdsmen as compared to the level of many land tilling peasants in the poorer regions of China. But if the movement is not stopped the grasslands will soon become as poor a place to live as any other impoverished region of China.

大 The Reform
回 Unravels:
潮 Rural Change 1986

After working for five months in China in 1986, I had a feeling that
conditions were not as stable as they had been the year before. The
whole country seemed far less stable, the problems more widespread
and urgent, and the government less capable of handling them.

The key weakness showed up in foreign trade. Sometime late last
year or early this year, Beijing authorities decided that certain cities
and whole provinces could make their own deals with foreign concerns.
The upshot was that Beijing lost control of the whole process, provinces
and cities began wheeling and dealing on a large scale, imports shot up,
and the country ran through half or more of its foreign currency
reserves in a few months. Much of the goods imported came from
Japan: cars, television sets, tape recorders, refrigerators. They flooded
the country from one end to the other and threatened the demise of
large sections of native industry. People began to talk of "a second
Japanese conquest of China."

Trade balances that had always heretofore been in China's favor
suddenly went against China, especially the trade balance with Japan.
Added to that was the serious corruption, such as the Hainan Island
scam, whereby officials imported thousands of mini-vans at high dollar
rates, then turned around and sold them to the rest of the country at
vastly inflated prices, making illegal profits for Hainan and for themselves. While all this was going on, inflation continued to mount,

This article is a revised version of a report prepared for the Ministry of Agriculture,
Animal Husbandry, and Fisheries, Peoples Republic of China, 1986.

95

forcing lots of prices up, especially food prices, vegetable prices, and meat prices. City people on fixed incomes found it harder and harder to make ends meet.

In September, students in Beijing finally took to the streets. A few thousand paraded in Tiananmen Square. The government acted quickly, mobilizing large numbers of youths to block the gates at Qinghua and other campuses, thus keeping further protests off the streets of the capital. But in the provinces, due to effective liaison between young people, students marched in many cities.

Trade Problems

On the surface the demonstrations were anti-Japanese. The immediate cause was the visit of Japan's premier to a Shinto shrine where he paid his respects to the memory of military men, including some who are regarded as war criminals in China. This shocked the Chinese, who are very sensitive to anything that looks like the remilitarization of Japan. Some recalled that Japanese aggression against China began with trade and investment. So the first slogans were "Down with the flood of Japanese goods" or "Stop the Japanese flood." The target shifted quickly to domestic issues, however. "Oppose inflation" and "Oppose corruption" led to much sharper phrases like "The government is incompetent," and "Down with the new Li Hongzhang."

Li Hongzhang was the Qing Dynasty viceroy who helped crush the Taiping Rebellion, brought in foreigners to build modern plants in China, built a so-called modern army and navy, lost the war to Japan in 1895, then gave in to humiliating Japanese demands at Shimoneseki. To call Deng the new Li Hongzhang is to criticize, first and foremost, his handling of Japan: Japanese trade, Japanese trade balances, imports, and investments. When a government loses control of imports and currency reserves it certainly becomes subject to charges of incompetence, particularly in China, in view of the history of China vis à vis imperialism in the last 150 years.

Of crucial importance in the sphere of trade has been the commitment of large quantities of Chinese resources as exports in order to balance up the import account. The new coal mine in Northwest Shanxi jointly exploited by Armand Hammer and the Chinese government, other big coal fields in North Shanxi and Inner Mongolia marked for export, and vast quantities of oil headed the same way have alarmed many people who fear that China is headed in a typical third world direction, giving up vast quantities of valuable resources at low prices for expensive industrial imports at the expense of building up its own industries. It would not take too many bad deals to put China in the same bind as Nigeria now finds itself—deep in debt peonage.

I heard many tales of native Chinese industries undercut by subsidized imports from abroad, imports that Chinese bought simply because they were foreign and not because they were superior to native products. My sister and her husband have been working for years to develop native Chinese dairy equipment. Now they have finally succeeded, but the whole effort is in jeopardy due to the export drives of Denmark, Japan, and Germany in this same sphere. Chinese state units would rather buy foreign than domestic, so they cut the throats of their own people. I also heard of a computer that Shenzhen could have bought from a firm in Chengdu, but bought from Italy instead because it was foreign. Thus the Chengdu firm had a hard time staying in business.

In the auto industry the foreign advantage is very clear. No one wants the Chinese cars. Every official wants to keep up with the Joneses by buying a Japanese car. My brother-in-law was worried that he wouldn't find his car and driver in front of the Beijing Hotel. But I pointed out to him that his unit's car was the only one, amidst hundreds of Japanese-made vehicles, that was made in Shanghai. He could pick it out anywhere. Why was his unit so backward? Because it was rural.

Those in the know said many bad deals are being made. If a foreign company can't put something over on government buyers or contract makers, they go below to provincial- or city-level units and make the rejected deal there. Thus they saddle China with a lot of shoddy equipment and outmoded technology. Since hi-tech is the craze, anything high-tech sells well even if it can't be used, even if China makes the same thing better.

Unloading the Burden of the Peasantry

In agriculture some surprising things are happening. Ironically, new developments are reviving under Deng, some tendencies that, when they occurred under Mao, became the target of Deng's sharpest criticism. For example, there is such a big exodus of labor from the land, so many millions of peasants abandoning tillage for local industries and sundry trades, that, just as during the Great Leap, the remaining labor force is unable to cope with the crops.

With returns for labor on the land falling so low, nobody wants to stay at home and farm. Communities have to subsidize agriculture with industrial earnings, which amounts to a great *ping diao*, or leveling and transferring of wealth. This grossly violates the principle of "to each according to work performed." It was cooperatives that were supposed to violate this principle, but now suddenly in the privatized rural community much of the village income from contracting out land and sideline enterprises has to be allocated as subsidies to those who agree to remain on the land. If this is not "leveling and transferring," what is it? We are back to "one big pot," which is a term of derision, used against the cooperatives. The more things change, the more they remain the same.

Community subsidies for agriculture involve amounts that are not small. In Long Bow village, where I spent four days, each field contractor gets 60 yuan per mu total. This consists of free plowing, free harrowing, free fertilizer, free seed, free pest control, and a subsidy of a nickel a jin (1.1 pound) above the state price for all grain produced. This adds up to about $120 (official rate) per acre, which is more than the U.S. government allocates for various farm programs that discourage production. Over the country as a whole the subsidy figures must be enormous. And they do not include the various subsidies which have been built into the grain procurement price ever since the 20 percent price increase back in 1980. I used to feel that whereas industrial Japan could subsidize domestic grain prices this was not possible in China, but apparently this is what is happening. Even a modest increase in mechanization would make it unnecessary, but so long as the main tillage implement remains the hoe, and the main harvest implement the sickle, farming will have to be subsidized wherever nonfarm employment opportunities are significant.

Of course, not all these phenomena are a bad thing. It is good that millions of peasants leave the land if they can settle into other productive pursuits. The drawing off of people, the difficulty of finding help, the sharp rise in wage rates, all create good conditions for mechanization, which is the only long-term solution to the problem. Unfortunately, the new regime is no better prepared than was the old to provide the needed machinery, so the labor problem is solved by migrants, vast flows of people from the poorer hill regions who come down to do the heavy work by the day and go home at the end of the season with a little stake.

I learned that this fall in Guangdong one had to pay 6 yuan a day for harvest labor in the fields, not counting the free meals, sorghum liquor, and cigarettes that the employer must also provide. Since it takes a peasant four full days of work to harvest a mu of rice, the cash outlay alone comes to close to 25 yuan. Twenty-five yuan per mu means 150 yuan per acre ($50 at the official rate; $25 at the market rate) just in harvest costs, not to mention the extras. This is way above machine harvest costs in the United States for crops of equivalent yield. And all this because of the rise in the price of labor due to sideline and industrial development.

Labor costs last fall amounted to 4 yuan per day in Sichuan, 10 yuan per day this fall in Heilongjiang, and from 3 to 5 yuan per day—but only 1.5 yuan per day for women—this fall in Shanxi. These are great increases over the past and point up the need for mechanization now rather than the open-ended expansion of a migrant labor market through which the richly endowed peasants of the plains exploit the poorly endowed hill people. Unfortunately, higher authorities ignore the problem.

A Functioning Collective

To see something quite different, we went to Wanggongzhuang, a village that copied Long Bow's mechanization and became so prosperous it refused to break up when the new policy was introduced. All the leaders disappeared every time the county authorities came down to find them. This went on until the break-up wind blew itself out after a year or two. So now Wanggongzhuang is one of the best mechanized and one of the most cooperative villages in all of China, and township leaders are mobilizing other villages to copy it. The experience is spreading far beyond the immediate locality, even though the achievements cannot be reported up to Beijing or even to Taiyuan, the provincial capital, because they are not in accord with policy.

The provincial machinery officials wrote my report for me, saying that the way forward for mechanization was through contracting larger tracts of land by crop production specialists. It is true that I did not oppose this route, so long as they find a way to mechanize soon, but I also advocated the Wanggongzhuang cooperative route organized around the "four unities." This latter route involves all land contractors in a joint effort, practicing unified planning, financing, management, and mechanization. Another list of the "four unities" presents them as: unified planning, unified purchasing, unified technology or technical measures, and unified machine work.

In other words, in these cooperative communities, even though the land has been contracted out, all the wheat is planted together, all the corn planted together, all the beans planted together. The community buys the finest grade seed and the best fertilizer, then a central machine group, either owned and managed by the community or contracted to a local specialist, does all the plowing, harrowing, fertilizing, planting, and spraying, right through until harvest time. All the individual family does is some crop care in the interim, in corn, perhaps, some light weeding or some detasseling (in South Shanxi they believe that detasseling two rows out of four increases yields 10–15 percent). Then at harvest time they keep the crop separate. Each family stores its own and each family keeps its own accounts, paying out whatever it owes for inputs and machine work.

This really represents a high degree of collectivization and a high degree of joint management. Where we saw it practiced the results were excellent. But it is a far cry from the privatization that is standard today throughout the Chinese countryside. And it is so out of line with state policy that the Shanxi machinery people did not want me to mention it as a possible road forward in my report.

The Wangongzhuang results are really impressive. They started with a lot of land per capita, at least for Shanxi, with 5,680 mu for 1,611 people, of whom some 455 are ablebodied. Their cropland equals 5,442 mu, or slightly more than half an acre per person. So even after handing out about a mu of per capita grain land to each man, woman, and child they still had a large acreage to farm commercially, to contract out but to manage jointly as was their custom. The yield picture looks like this:

Year	Yield Per Acre	
1978	46	bushels
1979	71	"
1980	88	"
1981	96	"
1982	103	"
1983	112	"
1984	118	"
1985	118+	"

This progress really began with mechanization, especially with the corn picker, which has a stalk chopper built in. Since the pickers chop up the stalks as they pick the ears, all organic residue goes back into the soil, enriching the fields from year to year. This gives the soil much greater water-holding capacity and makes the chemical fertilizer more available to plants. When you add to this the top-quality seed, the increased amounts of fertilizer, the addition of phosphate fertilizer to the usual nitrogen used, some use of herbicides for weed control and perhaps the detasseling, you get an unbeatable formula for raising production year after year. Since the machines liberated labor power this village, which could previously hardly handle the grain land, branched out into sidelines—processing, transport, livestock (particularly chicken raising), silk worms, silk filiatures, and construction crews—to push up income by 333 percent. Agriculture and sidelines combined now provide 418 yuan per capita per year as against 66 yuan in 1978.

Wanggongzhuang's success has inspired the whole township and the whole county, for that matter, and many other brigades have decided to follow its example. This method has the support of county leaders now, but no one can publicize the experience nationally or even at the province level because it is not in accord with policy.

The contrast between the remarkable results in Wanggongzhuang and the farming in other places is sharp. We saw peasants burning enormous quantities of stalks in the fields to make room for the planting of wheat. They burn the corn stalks and bean stalks wholesale in Southeast Shanxi in the fall, and after the summer harvest the wheat stalks or straw as well. All of this useful organic matter is burned because it is in the way and villages don't have enough labor power to process it by hand. Of course, traditionally they used to burn all these stalks as fuel for cooking and heating, but with the development of coal mining in recent decades and with coal so cheap everywhere in Shanxi, people burn coal as fuel and the stalks are no longer needed for domestic survival.

We saw places where the peasants had piled stalks along the highway embankments at the ends of the fields, then set them afire and burned them in such a way that the heat killed the shade trees that lined the highway. In late October universal burning filled the Shanxi air with smoke; one could smell it on the wind everywhere and see it on the horizon, an ubiquitous blue haze. A terrible, terrible waste!

Since privatization all the traditional threshing floors have turned out to be too small. Every family must now have its own space so all the contracting peasants, if they live anywhere near a highway, bring their unthreshed grain to the road, lay it out on the pavement to be thrashed by the vehicles passing through, then dry the grain on the shoulder of the road. Peasants have always used roads this way, but never on such a massive scale. This October we literally traveled several kilometers at a time over crops to be threshed. At one point bean stalks wrapped on our drive shaft and jammed it and it took about an hour to cut ourselves free.

The grain processed on the roads gets really dirty. Oil from the passing trucks, cars, and tractors, manure and urine from the horses and mules, tar from the blacktop underneath all contaminate the grain. Governments at various levels have forbidden processing on the roads again and again, but it still goes on on an ever more massive scale. No one can control it. To make sufficient threshing floors to substitute for these road areas would further deplete the amount of cropland and no one is in favor of that. Collective threshing uses much less space; it's the private threshing that bursts all bounds.

In north Shanxi we saw a county where privatization combined with good leadership had led to a big expansion of the dairy industry. Shanyin now boasts 8,000 cows, most of them privately owned but all descended from a 1,000-cow state herd that has been there for a long time. In one village we found 500 cows—two to a family, three to a family, one to a family—and each cow in milk can yield a profit of 2,000 yuan a year. The peasants raise corn and feed the cows corn meal and chopped stalks (the grain ration has added nutrients from a local mill);

they milk and after each milking send their milk to a milk powder plant by bicycle twice a day. What a sight! All those people, young and old, on bicycles with plastic containers of milk strapped on both sides of the rear wheel lining the roads on the way to the milk plant. There is no question that sideline development is the way to go and dairy cows, at least for now, are a profitable sideline. But the whole process leads to polarization and quite rapidly. Already the biggest private dairy has thirty head while the average family has but one or two. With thirty head you have to hire labor, at least one person for every three or four cows.

Everywhere we heard complaints about taxes and fees. The dairies were no exception. It seems that the Light Industry Bureau has the right to levy fees on all non-crop production regardless of origin, even if it makes no contribution toward setting up or managing the enterprise. For instance, as soon as you start to milk a cow a cent and a half of the 26 cents you get per jin of milk goes to the Light industry Bureau as a management fee. Another cent and a half goes in other taxes so three cents comes off (almost 12 percent) before the milk even reaches the plant. After that it is subject to various processing taxes, shipping taxes, and so on—a real burden on the farming communities. People resent it and they are talking about it.

Peasants who opt for transport on the road by buying a small tractor and trailer are subject to over twenty different fees—license fees, road use taxes, load taxes—you name it, there is a tax for it. These cut way down on the profitability of transport. Among the twenty they list insurance. This seems a reasonable charge, but many of the other charges are not reasonable at all. They have the appearance of feudal exactions, unwarranted restraints on trade imposed by local powerholders.

Cooperation Yields Success

In the Northeast, in Heilongjiang, mechanization, at least for tillage and planting, was quite widespread in the past. Peasants often used combines to harvest the small grains and the beans if not the corn. The reforms dealt mechanization a staggering blow. Of the 10,000 villages in Heilongjiang, only 181 retained collective control over machinery, that is, collective ownership and management. Twenty percent contracted their machinery to private operators and the rest, over 80 percent sold the machinery outright at sacrifice prices to those with an inside track—such as brigade leaders, their relatives, and friends. On the average the machinery brought only about one-third of its original price. If one assumes that depreciation had already exhausted a third of the value then the machinery sold at half price. However you figure it, it was a great rip-off of collective wealth, a major giveaway, and those who bought the machinery, having got it at such cheap prices, were often unprepared to pay for major repairs when the time came for that. They used the machinery, mainly tractors, plows, and a few combines, until the time came for repairs, then they abandoned it.

After reform most machinery did only a portion of the work it had done before. In almost every case the sales broke up implement sets so that the new owners could not contract any whole job, any whole crop sequence. One operator could plow for a peasant producer, another could harrow or plant, still a third might harvest, but no operator bought a complete set of crop production equipment. Thus utilization fell off sharply. Over the province as a whole, on the other hand, officials insisted that crop yields did not fall, but maintained fairly good levels. This is because the land contractors, doing the job primarily by hand or with draft animals are working a lot harder, putting in more and more intensive hours.

We visited two villages that were exceptions to the great sell-off rule. Both had refused to break up. Jianhua village had over 13 mu per capita and if you include range land, almost 26 mu per capita—about twelve times the national average. The Communist Party secretary decided on retaining ownership of the machinery and organizing its use through a mechanization team or teams. About ten families who thought they would get rich only if the coop broke up, left to seek their fortunes elsewhere. But the village, still functioning as a collective, did very well and this year the ten families came back and begged for readmission. The party secretary wisely invited them back and even organized a welcome home party for them. They returned because they found that it was not so easy to get rich on their own. The people who stayed home and worked together were doing much better financially.

This brigade had an impressive record in sidelines, with 50,000 chickens raised by scores of families (several hundred to several thousand to a flock), a large fresh-water fish industry using man-made ponds, an oil-processing plant, cattle-raising on range land, and many other projects. They also had a pretty high level of mechanization, including one large parallel sprinkler system that could water several thousand mu, primarily wheat land. The potential here seemed great, especially if they maintain collective control.

While north of Chichihar we went one day to a second, even larger village that Shandong people settled on wasteland some twenty years ago. Here the collective level was even higher than at Jianhua. The place was functioning as the most successful collectives functioned elsewhere in China in the past. The accumulation fund was large enough to allow for big investments so the brigade had its own powdered milk plant and its own fruit cannery. Members had their own orchards and their own evergreen tree plantations as well as a deer farm. They had also invested in three big city stores (two in Chichihar and one in Harbin) and a taxi company.

The central government man traveling with me asked the party secretary why he had not followed policy and contracted everything out. "I don't want to give you a long lecture on Marxism-Leninism," the party secretary said, "so I'll just give you three reasons: It wasn't practical to do it; we couldn't figure out a way to do it; and we didn't want to do it." He then elaborated on the three, with stress on the last. He himself was the manager of the off-farm enterprises and boasted he made money even while sleeping. He had set up a bonus system tied to off-farm enterprise profits and since the receipts far surpassed the plan in 1985 he was supposed to get 30,000 yuan personally. The average per capita income in this village is 1,700 yuan, 600 from private family projects, such as family cows, and 1,100 from collective projects. The party secretary projected that by 1988 total income would be about 7 million yuan—1 million from agriculture, 1 million from forestry, 1 million from livestock (mostly dairy cows) and 3 million from industries, trade, and outside enterprises, plus 1 million from private family earnings. This would create a per capita net income of 3,000 yuan.

This community had seventeen large tractors, five large combines, and dozens of implements of all kinds. With this machinery the cooperators farmed over 300 mu (50 acres) per laborer which is well over ten times the average in the Northeast. It would have been the height of folly to divide, yet tens of thousands of communities with mechanization approaching this level did divide. Singing the praises of these collective places does not get one anywhere now, however, because they are considered mavericks, out of line with policy. Yet they are much touted by the machinery people because they are continuing to demonstrate what cooperation plus machinery can do.

Elsewhere in the Northeast the machinery people are trying to make the best of a bad situation by pushing Machine Owners Associations, where those who have bought machinery or contracted exclusive rights to machinery will organize, coordinate, set rates and standards, and then provide effective custom work for the individual land contractors. But if the contractors, on their part, do not practice some form of "four unities" the effort will be in vain because there won't be any large pieces of land on which the machines can rationally function.

This year in the southern regions of the Northeast, in Liaoning, the rivers flooded badly. The Liao went over its banks in the rainy season and destroyed the crops over a wide area. The destruction was so great that city people in North China got nervous and began to horde grain tickets for the first time in several years. For a while, after the surpluses of 1984, it looked as if the private grain market would supply all the grain needed at bargain prices, but that clearly is no longer a probability. Suddenly rationing, grain coupons, and state guarantees look attractive again. Rumor had it that Guangdong fell short of grain and wanted to buy more from Hunan, but Hunan refused to allow the grain out since its leaders feared local shortages themselves. In the meantime the heavy rains in the lower Yangtze Valley just at harvest time caused a lot of grain there to rot. I guess it is no wonder that Chen Yun raised the grain question very sharply and called on the government to pay special attention to grain. The *China Daily* of December 12, 1985, reported a sharp drop in the national grain harvest, and follow-up report the next day said that half the land in Guangdong had been diverted to nonfarm use.

Grasslands Polarized

In the summer of 1986 I traveled all through Inner Mongolia looking at the grasslands and the deserts (it is sometimes hard to tell the difference). There I found the situation to be as serious as ever—

everywhere overgrazing and no real program to overcome the destruction. No matter where we went the people all said the grazing was worse than it had been ten years ago and much worse than in their childhood.

Yet even in the deserts, sparse as the population was, we saw the same social differentiation that we had seen elsewhere: bold contractors assume the use-rights to more property than they can work, then hire poorer neighbors to do the hard manual work. One man who had bought or somehow acquired a young orchard from his collective was temporarily growing watermelons between the apple trees with the help of three hired laborers. When we went to see the plots he ordered his laborers to find ripe melons for us to eat, then cut them up and gave his guests a copious share while the laborers looked on wistfully. He offered them nary a piece. I was reminded of the relationship between landlords and hired laborers in old China.

Where the government initiates dune fixation projects it often contracts them out. The state pays so much per mu of work. The insiders contract the acreage, then hire neighbors to do the hard manual work and pocket the difference. Thus the polarization spreads even on the wide frontier. A Mongolian friend said, "labor-management relations have returned to the stage of primitive capitalism as described by Karl Marx." When I asked what that meant, he said, "The owners have all the rights and the workers none. It's hire, fire, squeeze, and exploit without hindrance or organized resistance."

We went to an entirely different area in the central Ordos where the water table lay hundreds of feet down and the wells were few and far between. The wells that did exist were generating small concentric deserts because so many thousand head of stock had to concentrate around each for water. While visiting one well we learned that the only other well in the neighborhood, one drilled by the local collective at a cost of 10,000 yuan, had been bought by one individual for 3,000 yuan. This herdsman bought it for 30 cents on the dollar and was using it to enhance his personal fortune. In that same area we saw farm machinery—things like fodder choppers for silage making, large mowing machines, and large electric generators—abandoned, stripped, and rusting, the copper wire ripped from the generators. Everything is private now and the scale is too small to put such machinery to work.

The biggest single contract that I saw anywhere in the grasslands was for 20,000 mu. An Atakachi man with a rather large extended family had contracted this large area (some 3,000 acres), had borrowed money from the bank, and had fenced off about half of it. He had also contracted with the collective for the use of the hay baler—a 10,000 yuan machine—and was making hay on the unfenced uplands. In haying season he hired several laborers. There was still some grass up there because there was no water available for grazing herds to drink.

The officials told me that in the entire area there were about five contracts for over 10,000 mu. Most of them, however, were in the 2,000 to 3,000 mu range and many were for 1,000 mu or less. I think the 20,000 mu man is bound to do well, but what will the 1,000 mu fellows do? There, as elsewhere, the range looked badly depleted. It was already the end of the rainy season, the very best time of year for grass, but hardly a blade of grass could be seen. Whatever showed green turned out to be unpalatable weeds that no stock wanted to eat and between these weeds bare soil showed all around.

Waste Slopes, Virgin Grass

Going over the mountains north of Hohhot and in the northern part of the Ordos we saw millions of mu of badly eroded slopes. The hills look as if they are being torn apart by the claws of giant tigers. The authorities do not call these regions grasslands, although if left to themselves they might be covered with grass; they call them waste slopes. We saw hardly any trees. In Inner Mongolia, they say, if you want to hang yourself you have to walk 100 miles to find a tree.

Since here and there the hills are broken by small gullies and flats that peasants can cultivate, they class these lands as agricultural. The peasants till the barren plots, then run as many head of stock as possible on the hills. No one has a plan or a program to control the grazing, revive the hills, or check the terrible erosion. When I asked what measures could possibly save the day our guide looked at me in amazement. "But these are waste slopes," he said. It was clear that nobody had any plans for them at all. I don't mean to imply that the plans they have for the other grasslands are effective, but at very least a lot of people are worrying about their future. Most people recognize that there is a problem and they hold lots of discussions and lots of meetings and conduct lots of studies. Not so for the waste slopes. Yet a quarter of all the livestock in Inner Mongolia graze on the waste slopes!

East of Xilinhot—two days journey to the east, not far from the Outer Mongolian border—we actually did see some undergrazed rangeland, on the western slope of the Greater Kingan Mountains. The lands had not been grazed primarily because the water table was so low—down several hundred feet—so stock could come in only in winter when there was snow on the ground to slake thirst. Here we even saw natural forests and some of the most beautiful wild country that I have ever seen anywhere—most of it not forested but grass covered—huge rolling ridges clothed in grass from bottom to top and stretching away to the horizon in an endless velvet carpet. In this whole region we saw only one herd, mixed cattle and sheep. When we started to take pictures our guide protested. "Don't photograph those animals," he said. "They are poaching. They come from south of the mountains." They came from Balin Right, which I visited in 1983, from a range even more heavily overgrazed than most ranges in Xilinhot. So Balin Right's desperate herdsmen even braved the waterless mountains to find some virgin grass.

The Kingan Mountain area was indeed a paradise, but it comprises only a small fraction of the total grassland. Nevertheless, it is large enough to give rise to the myth of great untapped resources on the frontier of the nation. If the government ever stopped building high-rises in Beijing long enough to send a little capital for well-drilling to the Kingan range then that whole range would soon be depleted also, because if herdsmen could find water there they would soon load the mountains with livestock enough to finish everything off. In some ways, then, it is lucky that there is little money for agricultural development in China now.

大回潮 Bypassed by Reform: Agricultural Mechanization 1986

Today there is much talk about the modernization of China. Thousands are traveling abroad to study the latest technology; industrial ministries import the most up-to-date equipment for coal mining, steel making, transportation, electronic appliance manufacture; and computers are all the rage. The "information revolution" excites the imagination of the younger generation. But there is one whole sphere that everyone leaves out, and that is the mechanization of agriculture. In the great reorganization of the government that took place during the early years of the reform only one set of institutions disappeared, those dealing with agricultural mechanization. The officials who staffed them only managed to survive as functionaries by creating semigovernmental, semicommercial units with such names as "Agricultural Mechanization Service Station" and titles such as "Station Head." China, it seems, is willing to modernize everything but the physical labor involved in crop production. Still, a big question remains: Can China modernize without mechanizing agriculture?

Modernization, if it means anything at all, must mean the modernization of production and the heart of modern production has to be a high level of labor productivity. Without high productivity how can one speak of a modern economy, modern science and technology, or modern defense? And since agricultural production is still a major sector of the total economy, if not the major sector, labor productivity in agri-

This article is a revised and shortened version of a letter written to Neville Maxwell, one of the founders of the Society for Anglo-Chinese Understanding, in March 1985.

culture must also be modernized. Modern industry, science, and technology cannot develop for long on the foundation of a primitive agriculture. An economy that is half-modern, half-primitive is a contradiction in terms. Backwardness in the countryside undermines the smooth development of other spheres, of industry, and of the whole society.

The key to labor productivity in agriculture is mechanization. Without mechanization labor power cannot leave the land to take up other types of production. Without mechanization tillers on the land cannot produce enough to afford industrial products. Without mechanization, peasants slip into the category of second-class citizens who cannot gain a foothold in modern society because they cannot produce or, as a consequence, consume enough to qualify as participants.

Current policymakers in China propose to improve agricultural productivity thorough implementation of the "responsibility system," combined with so-called scientific farming. By "scientific farming" they mean improving the genetic makeup of plants and animals, promoting better and more complete fertilizers, applying advanced pest control measures, and paying attention to careful field management, multiple cropping systems, interplanting systems, close planting, deep tillage, and fine tillage.

On the one hand this "scientific farming" is supposed to increase yields per acre or hectare. The family contract system, on the other hand, is supposed to raise labor productivity by providing direct material incentive for hard and skillful work.

The reformers downplay, even ignore, agricultural mechanization. The new Five Year Plan (1986–90) mentions mechanization only once, in passing, as something that should be supported, rather like being for virtue and against sin. But scientific farming coupled with hard work cannot hope to solve the problem of productivity on the land. Crop yields in China are already comparatively high. Science and hard work may double yields, they may even triple yields, but it is unlikely that they can quadruple yields. Yet even if by such methods peasants in China could quadruple their yields their productivity as crop producers would still lag far behind world levels. This is true because, in the first place, applying these so-called scientific measures almost always requires additional labor input which offsets, to some extent, the effect of the gain in yield as it relates to labor productivity. And because, in the second place, the productivity gap is so enormous, China must raise productivity not two, four or six times to catch up with the modern world, but several hundred times, as can be seen from Table 1 and Table 2:

Table 1. Labor days (10 hour days) Per Mu of Corn Harvested

US (Pennsylvania)	.037 (no-till)
	.08 (conventional till)
China (Shandong) Dongliang village, Chaoyuan County	11.40
Yeji village, Huang County	15.00

Table 2. Labor days (10 hour days) Per Ton of Corn Produced

US (Pennsylvania)	0.077 (no-till)
	0.156 (conventional till)
China (Shandong) Dongliang village, Chaoyuan County	38
Yeji village, Huang County	33

Looking at the comparative figures for corn production in Pennsylvania and Shandong, we can see that (1) the average Pennsylvania farmer tills from 142 to 405 times as much land as the average peasant in a relatively advanced Shandong village, yet harvests comparable yields; and (2) the average Pennsylvania farmer produces from 213 to 438 time as much grain per labor day as the average peasants in a relatively advanced Shandong village. The only way to redress the balance, to close the gap, is mechanization, and mechanization must be included under the application of "science."

Mechanization not only can be defined as a major aspect of the modern science of tillage or crop production, but by itself, promotes scientific farming in numerous ways. For example, soil organic matter must be increased to promote water absorption, water holding capacity, and by the same token the availability of fertilizer in the soil. Yet currently peasants commonly burn straw and stalks to get them out of the way of the following crop. And this is because they do not have enough labor power to dispose of them in any other way. Without machines for chopping straw and stalks and without machines for turning them under they have to burn them. This practice threatens yields. Adequately powered machines also promote timely tillage, timely planting, uniform seed spacing, seed depth, fertilizer placement, and herbicide and insecticide application—often all in one pass across the field. All these factors promote high yields.

The Problem of Unemployment

The most common objection to any proposal for agricultural mechanization is that there is already much too much labor power in the countryside and that any labor released by mechanization cannot find alternative employment. Mechanization, so conventional wisdom affirms, must create unemployment, which is unacceptable.

This objection oversimplifies the problem. While in the country as a whole, there may be, and probably is, a surplus of agricultural labor, locally there are many parts of China that lack labor power or will soon lack labor power for farm work. Wherever the economy is developing fast, wherever sidelines and small industries are expanding rapidly, large numbers of peasants are leaving the land, labor shortages are developing, and wages are rising steeply. In 1986 in some parts of Heilongjiang province, farm hands were earning 10 yuan a day—far more than most workers in Beijing industrial plants. In Guangdong harvest hands were earning 6 yuan a day plus meals, cigarettes, and wine. In Beijing suburban districts, migrant rice transplanters were getting from 6 to 15 yuan a day and even at these rates good workers were hard to find because nobody wants to do stoop labor in the paddies any more. Low labor productivity on the land coupled with expanding economic opportunity off the land causes a number of problems.

First, ablebodied laborers seek higher earnings elsewhere, which means that the less productive workers, the old, the young, the weak, and the female remain on the land as the main force. A depleted labor force does not farm well, resulting in low yields, and land is abandoned by peasants who are unable to cope.

Partly as a result of the reduced labor force, moreover, the agricultural infrastructure—terrace walls, drainage ditches, irrigation channels, river dykes, wind breaks, and forest belts—is neglected. Straw and stalk composting is sharply reduced along with night soil gathering and many other labor intensive practices essential to high, sustained yields.

Finally, without the sharing of sideline and industrial profits which collectives used to guarantee through the sharing of workpoints team-by-team, peasants are reluctant to contract land for commercial farming. Many communities must therefore still guarantee free seed, free fertilizer, free plowing, and bonus prices for grain before anyone will assume a contract. This diverts community resources that could be invested in expanded reproduction right back into ordinary farm production and thus holds back development. It amounts to a form of *ping diao*—the Chinese word for leveling and transferring wealth—from efficient to inefficient producers, something the responsibility system was supposed to get away from. Far from getting away from this, however, the new system has only reproduced it in a new form. And where do the communities get the money for this? They get it from the contract fees that individuals pay for the use of industrial and commercial properties and assets. Industry supports agriculture after all.

Many well-organized, well-managed villages in rapidly developing areas feel the labor pinch acutely. In Dongliang village, Chaoyuan county, Shandong, which has 1,600 ablebodied laborers, village leaders project that by 1990 they will lack 473 workers. This is because they are planning to create several new industries. They want to release the needed workers from the fields with a higher level of mechanization.

Yeji village, Huang county, Shandong, which has 1350 ablebodied workers, projects a shortage of 213 by 1990. Yeji leaders also want to release hundreds from the fields with mechanization. Only mechanization can solve these problems. A moderate investment in new machinery can raise productivity by a multiple of ten right away. This machinery can also raise yields, lower unit production costs, and encourage some of the best ablebodied workers to stay on the land instead of leaving it.

Labor shortages are evident in regions of three different types: (1)

rural areas where sidelines, small industries and mining are expanding rapidly; (2) rural areas on the outskirts of most large and many medium-sized cities; and (3) rural areas where land is plentiful and people are few—the Northeast, the Northwest, and Inner Mongolia. Together these areas add up to more than 30 percent of China.

In areas of the first two types the transfer of labor into sidelines, small industries, and mines, creating shortages and raising wage rates, has created very favorable conditions for mechanization. There profits from nonagricultural production, accumulated by collectives and by individuals also ensure investment funds.

However, in these areas, mechanization is difficult due to the complexity and variety of the cropping systems, the variety of the crops, the current small size of the fields, and the many special situations that require the invention of new types of machinery or the radical adaptation of old types. The people and units concerned have not done nearly enough research and development work to determine the type of machines and implements needed and cannot supply effective sets of mechanization tools any time soon. Social and economic developments have outpaced all technical efforts.

In areas of the third type, in contrast, mechanization is comparatively easy because machines imported from Europe and North America can be put to work with little modification. The prototypes already exist. The main problem here is lack of capital.

Mechanization should begin immediately in areas of these three types because conditions are ripe and the demand is great. But whenever such action is proposed people always raise the problem of the mountainous areas, the hillside rice areas, the backward loess highlands, and other difficult to mechanize regions, implying that mechanization should not begin anywhere unless it can be applied everywhere. But the truth of the matter is that the mechanization of the more advanced and more easily mechanized areas will be a tremendous boon to the poor, backward, mountainous areas once they too have created the social conditions, primarily the alternative employment opportunities, for reducing the farm labor force. A wide variety of tractors and implements will by then already exist, most of the options necessary will already be available and most production problems will already have been solved. Clearly the policy should be "Let some areas mechanize first." This will clear the way for those who follow.

Problems of Scale and Scope

Once a commitment to mechanization is made, a decision must be taken regarding what size of machinery should take precedence. Should China concentrate efforts on creating implements for small, 15-horsepower walking and four-wheeled tractors and depend on such equipment for future production or concentrate effort on creating implements for medium-sized 40–100 horsepower tractors and depend on them for the future?

Some people argue that since so many small walking and four-wheeled tractors have been produced and since so many peasants already own them they should be the mainstay of the mechanization effort. In my opinion, this would be a very impractical course. Too many farm tasks are beyond the power of these machines. Deep plowing, heavy discing, deep chiseling, land leveling, stalk chopping, manure hauling and spreading, corn picking, and many other harvest chores cannot be done or can only be done at heavy cost with low horsepower machines. Already yields are suffering because small tractors cannot plow more than a few inches deep. Shallow hardpans are forming just below the surface that these same small tractors cannot break up.

It would make much more sense to make medium-sized tractors in the 40–100 horsepower range the mainstay of China's mechanization. Such tractors, well supplied with complete sets of implements, can do a whole range of farm jobs from tillage to harvesting with a relatively high level of efficiency. Communities should put land together in blocks to make their work rational.

Each medium-sized tractor, well equipped, can handle from 1000 to 2000 mu of regular crop land, perhaps somewhat less of paddy rice. Since most villages in the north have from 1000 to 4000 mu of crops such medium-sized sets are suited to a management scale that still exists or can easily be revived. Planning can be done on a village-wide basis with mechanization teams or mechanization specialists providing land contractors with a wide variety of services. In such a scheme there will still be a place for the small walking and four-wheeled tractors that can provide field transport, spot spraying and other random light services.

The heart of the matter remains: mechanization, to be successful, must have some scale. To go all out at the 15 horsepower level is to condemn China to a chronically backward agriculture.

Another issue concerns the seasonal focus of mechanization: Should China focus on mechanization of rush season work or strive for the all-around mechanization of farm tasks? There is a strong bias in China for mechanizing only the rush season jobs, the jobs that clearly strain the labor capacity of the community. In my view this is shortsighted. The only way to truly liberate manpower is through the all-around mechanization of farm tasks. The whole production process of each crop should be mechanized. Only thus can farming specialists or mechanization teams contract ever larger areas of cropland while others transfer time and attention elsewhere.

All-around mechanization can raise labor productivity many times over in a short time and can simultaneously greatly increase the hours worked per machine, especially the hours worked per tractor, thus reducing the costs of ownership and spreading depreciation over far more performance. Tractors should be supplied with enough equipment, enough implements so that they can not only plow, fit, and plant land, but also spread fertilizer before, during, and after planting, spray herbicides and insecticides, pile, turn, haul, and spread manure and compost, harvest a wide variety of crops, chop and spread stalks, level land, and so on.

Variety and Flexibility Needed

Technically, all-around mechanization is not very difficult, but some general warnings should be heeded:

First, China should not try to "reinvent the wheel."—that is, China should try out what has already been invented in the world first, altering it and modifying it to suit Chinese conditions wherever necessary. Chinese agriculture is complex and varied, but for almost every operation now done by hand there is already a fairly efficient machine at work in the world.

Second, China should be willing to change tillage and cropping methods to suit machine cultivation requirements that are reasonable. Many technicians and many peasants put up strong resistance to this idea, insisting that the machine do exactly what the peasant does by hand even though there is no scientific evidence that this or that particular hand method is better or results in higher yields or in a better quality crop. Thus many people insist on placing manure and compost in the hill, under the seed of both corn and wheat, something that is very difficult to do by machine, even when all evidence shows that broadcasting manure and compost and working it into all the ground produces equal, if not better, results.

Peasants should be educated and mobilized by effective demonstrations to accept:

(a) Row widths suited to machine cultivation. The main determinant here is the width of the tractor and/or implement tire that must pass between the rows.

(b) Precision planting that requires no thinning. This must be coupled with radical seed quality improvement since the method requires seed of proven germination.

(c) Seed drilling rather than seed placed in hills.

(d) Broadcast or drilled fertilizer in place of hill placement.

(e) Some minimum and even no-till where suitable. No-till has proven particularly advantageous where corn or beans follow winter wheat on the North China Plain. Planting without tilling prevents water logging after heavy rains and cracking when the soils dry out.

(f) Dry planted rice.

(g) The combining of crops that yield straw. Peasants always say they don't want the straw mashed by a combine, but very little straw is actually used for weaving, braiding or plaiting. Where straw is so used special measures must be taken.

(h) New cropping systems such as three crops in two years instead of two crops in one year and less intercropping. Guided by the idea that labor costs practically nothing and is everywhere in surplus, extension specialists in China have almost invariably promoted multicropping and intercropping practices that make enormous demands on labor even when there is very little sound evidence that the practice makes for better results. In Japan recently, farmers converted large areas of double cropped land to single crop long season rice and raised the yield per hectare. The same thing happened when peasants abandoned triple cropping for double in Sichuan.

Third, China should strive to provide as many options as possible on all basic machines. Most combines can handle up to thirty different crops. For each crop some special equipment may be necessary—special headers, special cylinders, special chaffers and screens, straw choppers, wheel weights, tracks in place of wheels, wide wheels or narrow wheels, and so on. Currently machines and implements come with very few options. When peasants try them and they don't work well they assume that machines cannot do the job. Such experiences greatly inhibit the development of mechanization.

China plants row crops with various spacings, depending on the region, the crop, and the intercrop. Tractors and implements should be made with easily adjustable wheels for wide tracking, narrow tracking, and everything in between, including single front wheel steering. All planters, cultivators, harvesters etc. should be made so that they can be adjusted for various row widths, crop heights, and other special conditions.

Fourth, to assure variety the farm machinery industry should plan on small runs of diverse products. Industry should not expect to or plan to make endless copies of any single prototype. Modern automated machine tools can easily be adapted to small runs, model changes, variations on a basic pattern. Instead of retooling, modern factories reprogram. In Japan private families own automated machine tools and contract small runs from large plants. The heart of the matter is flexibility.

Finally, China should not consider a problem solved just because one solution has been found, one prototype created. China urgently needs two-way plows for irrigated land, subsoil plows for hard pan, light, tractor mounted corn pickers for small fields and many other implements commonly used abroad. The goal of the farm machinery industry should be to provide diverse options so that peasants in many different regions growing many different crops can solve their unique cropping problems.

Appropriate Social Organization

Most important is the problem of what overall social and political organizations can best promote mechanization. In 1985 and 1986 I visited a number of advanced villages with above average mechanization levels. Every one of them has a strong collective core. They carry out most important steps in production through a central mechanization team organized by the community or through a contracting specialist and pay the team or contractor for work done at piecework rates. Individual families contract all the fields but personally carry out only certain phases of field management—flood irrigation, side dressing of fertilizer, or hand spraying. The mechanized activity determines yields, in the main, and not the lesser manual activities. Hence yields tend to be both high and uniform.

I feel that the most appropriate form for mechanization is a strong village collective that coordinates the work of all contracting families, draws up a uniform cropping plan, supplies all necessary inputs through joint buying, and provides machine services from a centrally owned or controlled center. Such a system combines individual responsibility with collective strength. It practices four unities, mentioned by almost all the communities I visited: (1) unified planning; (2) unified purchase of seed, fertilizer, pesticides, and other inputs; (3) unified application of technical measures; and (4) unified allocation and operation of machinery. With such a system peasants can achieve scale in crop production, can plant large areas of one crop together, and can deploy machinery economically.

The only alternative to this is to encourage farming specialists to contract larger and larger tracts on their own and purchase their own machinery. But even a 600 mu tract is too small to warrant a complete set of machinery. If any community chooses the specialist route it still must consider the creation of a central machinery group to do custom work for the specialists. Either that or several specialists must get together and share the necessary equipment, a difficult form of cooperation. Between the two forms the first has greater potential for development, now and in the future. The second is more difficult to create, to organize, and to sustain. It is far less stable.

If the government grants subsidies or credits to stimulate mechanization it should make them available to collectives as well as to individuals. It should not discriminate against collectives as is often the case now.

Next to rural organization the most important problem is costs. Most people consider mechanization to be much too expensive for peasants to undertake. However, complete sets of equipment to handle a wheat-corn-peanut rotation can be supplied for a capital investment of between 100 and 150 yuan per mu. This does not include irrigation equipment. (At the official rate the Chinese yuan exchanges at 3.72 to the U.S. dollar but the actual rate which is now available to certain units at foreign exchange markets is around 7 to the dollar.)

With depreciation figured at seven years and interest figured at 8 percent ownership cost would then run about 22–33 yuan per mu per year. Since many villages already have much basic equipment, especially for tillage, they would not need that much total new investment.

Mechanization costing 22–33 yuan per year (ownership cost) can save up to twenty days labor per mu. With labor priced at 3 yuan a day, that is 60 yuan. In addition, one can expect a fair increase in crop yield due to organic matter build-up, timeliness, and uniformity.

Forms of Government Support

To promote mechanization the government should consider adopting some of the measures used by the U.S. government in support of farm mechanization since World War II. At one time, for example, federal tax regulations rewarded anyone who invested heavily in productive equipment. For many years the government offered investment credit that in proportion to the investment made, cut down heavily on income taxes due. Producers found it advantageous to buy new equipment rather than turn money over to the government in taxes.

In addition, the U.S. government directly subsidized technical innovations useful to environmental preservation. For example, the Agricultural Stabilization and Conservation Service paid about one-third of the cost of no-till planters during the 1970s. This agency also made loans on grain in on-farm approved storage so that farmers could pay production expenses without selling grain at low harvest-time prices; farmers paid off the loans when they sold their grain, but if prices fell below the loan rate the government bought the grain. Through the Production Credit Association, moreover, the government granted credit for equipment purchases at reasonable rates to be amortized over seven years.

Over the years the U.S. government adopted many financial measures affecting prices, credits, taxes, and other economic factors that helped farmers stay in business. These included the promotion of exports, the buying of surpluses, direct production subsidies, and direct crop reduction subsidies.

While none of the measure may be suitable for China, China does need to adopt policies that will support not only agricultural production but also agricultural mechanization. A number of problems need attention now.

First is the price of farm equipment. Currently, manufacturers, by government decree, price farm equipment at disastrously low levels. The farm equipment industry cannot make money at such rates, consequently no one wants to manufacture farm equipment. The low prices are designed to aid peasants, but they are hard on the industry so in the long run peasants have little or nothing to buy. Perhaps the subsidy should go, instead, directly to the purchaser, while the industry charges competitive prices.

Custom charges for machine work also need remedying. In the past, the prices that farm machinery operators charged for plowing, planting, reaping, and combining were set far too low. They hardly covered the cost of the operation, not to mention depreciation and debt service on the machinery. As a result, as old machinery wore out, no one could afford new machinery. Even though custom work prices have recently been deregulated, the tradition of charging very low prices for such services to peasants still persists in many places.

Finally, agricultural piece-work and flat rate standards need to be adjusted. These should follow actual practice, not attempt to set practice, which tends to obstruct creativity and innovation.

Finding the right equipment for the various agricultural regions in China will require investment and planning. The authorities should select demonstration villages in each crop zone and there test out machinery in actual production. Technicians should select the best equipment for the purpose from all over the world, including China, and concentrate it in these centers to be tested, modified, and proven. Almost all tractors and implements now produced in China are of models long outdated. Most, based on U.S. prototypes from the 1930s, came from the USSR in the 1950s. Why should China produce up-to-date atuomobiles, ships, trains, planes, rockets, factory, mining, and construction equipment, yet still turn out farm equipment from the 1930s? Most of these models are both clumsy and fragile, plagued with both design and quality problems. They often give mechanization a bad name. If agriculture is the base why not build a solid, efficient modern base?

In order to mechanize agriculture smoothly measures must be taken to coordinate industry with agriculture. Currently those who make farm equipment don't use it, sell it to the end user or service it and those who use it don't make it. Industry offers only a few prototypes on a take-it-or-leave-it basis. Model changes are slow and far between. Factories take no responsibility once the equipment leaves their door.

In Europe and North America the manufacturer must both sell and service what he makes. Company field men and dealers under contract follow up each sale with service, parts, and advice. There is constant two-way interchange between farmer and dealer and farmer and company either through the dealer or directly through field representatives. The livelihood of both company and dealer depend on customer satisfaction, on quality, on service, and on the quality of service.

China should find ways to link manufacturer and user more closely. More local autonomy for the manufacturer and less *ding xing* would help. *Ding xing,* or "setting the form," the official approval of all designs prior to making allocation of materials, tends to create extreme rigidity throughout the industry and inhibits the development of the diversity which China must have for mechanization. Mechanization is on the verge of rapid expansion. Labor shortages and high wages in certain parts of China are pushing people toward the use of farm machinery. The peasants are generally ahead of the government and of industry on this question.

The ministries, bureaus, and units concerned should seize the time, solve the problem of creating complete sets for all-around mechanization and take the lead in the modernization of farming. Money must be appropriated, foreign exchange approved, prototypes imported, tests and trials conducted. This is a big task on today's agenda.

大回潮 Dazhai Revisited: 1987

Dazhai is a mountain village in Shanxi province that Mao Zedong chose as a model of rural development, primarily because it practiced cooperation and self-reliance. This small community of eighty families turned a barren, gully-scarred mountainside into rich, terraced farmland with irrigated yields that rivaled Iowa's. Dazhai peasants planted apple, walnut, and mulberry trees, raised silkworms, honey bees, chickens, and fat pigs, built a brick kiln, a bean noodle plant, a bauxite mine, and used the income from their crops and shops to build solid, stone housing for every family, educate both children and adults, and provide medical care for all.

After Mao's death Deng Xiaoping and his colleagues repudiated Dazhai, denounced its accomplishments as fraudulent and finally, in 1983, carried out from above the complete reorganization of the village. Newly appointed leaders drawing salaries from the state contracted its collectively built and collectively worked fields to individual families for private operation. Since then, the reformers claim, Dazhai residents have prospered mightily. They have increased crop yields, opened flourishing new sidelines, raised per capita incomes, and raised living standards. Dazhai, according to a recent story in *Xinhua News* (September 17, 1987), now demonstrates the superiority of the "responsibility system" over the cooperative egalitarianism of the past.

All this sounds plausible.

This article originally appeared in *Monthly Review* 39, no. 10 (March 1988).

Unfortunately for the credibility of *Xinhua News,* on-the-spot investigations fail to support the main thrust of the story. I have been to Dazhai many times in the last fifteen years, five times while the village still served as a collective model and four times after it suffered repudiation and underwent various stages of reform. Several of these visits were prolonged and intensive. The last was a one-day stopover in June 1987. My sister, Joan Hinton, followed this up with a longer stay in August.

Conclusion: since 1979 the Chinese media have consistently misrepresented Dazhai, disparaging collective achievements on the one hand and idolizing reform achievements on the other, with equal disregard for facts in both cases.

Biased Comparisons

Today's reports credit reform at Dazhai with:

—A sharp rise in gross income. Overall returns of 185,000 yuan in 1978 grew to 650,000 yuan in 1986.

—A sharp rise in per capita income. The average disposable income per person grew from 186 yuan in 1978 to 650 yuan in 1985. (However, disposable income fell to 608 in 1986 due to heavy investment in a second coal mine.)

—The creation of new money-earning enterprises and industries. Together they brought in over 490,000 yuan in 1986.

Close examination of these claims is revealing—and more for what they leave out than for what they include.

First, none of the yuan figures given are corrected for inflation.

The Chinese yuan has depreciated greatly since 1978. If one takes the official rate of exchange between the yuan and the U.S. dollar, the figures show a sharp decline in relative value from 1.6 yuan to the dollar in 1978 to 3.7 yuan to the dollar today. These official rates probably do not reflect the real decline of the yuan vis-à-vis the dollar. The black market rate is now closer to 6 or 7 than to 3.7. Nor do the figures take into account the decline of the dollar itself.

If one rates the yuan against a representative list of commodities on sale in China, the deterioration is also substantial. The yuan today will buy less than half the goods it bought in 1978. In Shanxi province a few years ago, corn sold for 9 cents a jin. Today it sells for 24 cents. Official figures from the November 9 *China Daily* describe a 27 percent jump in prices between 1985 and 1987 alone. To make figures comparable across the board, all 1978 figures ought to be at least doubled or all 1986 figures halved.

Second, prereform and postreform figures cannot be directly compared. They describe different things.

Whereas in the postreform period money income represents most of the income received, in the prereform period money income (paid out as cash or as grain with a fixed cash value) made up only 60 to 75 percent of total income. Brigade members, as shareholders in the collective, received most or all of their housing, medical care, fuel, electricity, and other goods and services free. The total value of these fringe benefits is hard to estimate, but figured at prereform prices it must be counted as worth at least 50 yuan per capita per annum. While today's contracting members still enjoy some fringe benefits, the relative contribution of the latter to total income is far less.

In assessing prereform incomes, furthermore, one must take into account the value of the newly created liquid assets added annually to the accumulation fund and the value of the fixed assets created by joint labor in capital construction, which occupied the labor force for many months every year. These assets were mainly high-yield, terraced fields and solid, calamity-proof stone caves for family homes. The fields brought no immediate return but ensured a higher level of earned income in the future. While it is difficult to give a monetary value to such assets, from the labor expended per mu and from the cash value per mu of fertile crop land and the cash value of cave homes, one can estimate that they were worth at least an additional 50 yuan per capita per annum.

To make a valid comparison one would have to add all these figures together: $186 + 50 + 50 = 286$, then double the sum to correct for inflation. The answer, 572, approaches the current per capita figure of 650. [1]

To be fair, the increased collective assets of present-day Dazhai should also be figured into the current per capita income figures. They would surely raise them by a significant amount. The figures, however, would not rise as high as one might expect because in the past winter

---

1. Many peasants of course prefer cash in hand and the possibility of television sets, tape recorders, and washing machines to increased fixed assets in land or houses. Nevertheless these assets cannot be ignored.

labor done for workpoints created the new assets. Today all community work such as fixing roads, repairing terraces, building new fields, extending irrigation, and adding new enterprises must be paid for with money wages.

Workpoints entitle a participant only to a proportionate share of that part of community income that is set aside for distribution as individual earnings. The more workpoints the labor force as a whole expends on capital construction, the less each point is worth because the work yields no income in the current year. By working on capital construction all winter an individual peasant can increase his or her share of the total fund distributed, as compared to the share of someone who does not join the work. But the work done will not increase the overall size of the fund, for that is determined by the value of the crops harvested and also by the income of sideline enterprises minus production expenses and funds set aside for welfare and for future expenses and investments. These latter two categories usually are combined in an accumulation fund.

Money wages, on the other hand, must be paid out of the accumulation fund, thus transferring wealth from the community to the individual. As the value of the fixed assets goes up, the liquid assets held in the accumulation fund go down. Furthermore, the wages earned should already be figured into the per capita income figure. None of this was true in the past.

In the past, also, all production expenses were clearly defined and accounted for. They were deducted from net income before the village set aside the welfare fund, the accumulation fund, and the distribution fund. Today, with almost all production in private hands, it is impossible to get a breakdown of production expenses. No one will volunteer any information. Of the 630,000 yuan of gross income in 1986, 306,000 went to individuals and it is this figure, divided by 504, that gives the per capita average earning of 608 for that year. However, it stands to reason that a certain amount of production expenses have to come out of this 306,000. The village pays for seed, fertilizer, insecticides, water, electricity, and plowing, if the latter is done by village tractor. Peasants still own their own tools, many own implements and draft animals, while eight own four-wheeled tractors and six own trucks. These privately owned tools, draft animals, tractors, and trucks all run up depreciation, repair (or veterinary) upkeep, and operations costs.

While some of these, such as fuel, may already be accounted for, others, such as fodder, certainly have not been. They must be deducted from the net income figures of the families involved, thus shrinking the per capita income averages reported for postreform Dazhai.

An additional small but significant difference between pre and post 1983 village accounts arises from the unprecendented addition of the village party secretary to the state payroll, thus relieving the village of the burden of supporting him. Since no Dazhai resident would agree to carry out privatization policy, the government, in December 1982, sent a state cadre in to implement the decisions of a county reform work team. Since then the township has paid the salary of the Communist Party secretary. The man who currently holds the job gets 700 yuan per year, plus 3 yuan per day when talking to visitors. By August 1987 he had earned over 270 yuan from this source alone. Since he also has the use of a plot of land he earns something from the crops as well.

In the minds of Dazhai people any salary from the state places a person on the far side of a great divide that separates peasants, who live off their own hard physical labor, from those who do other kinds of work. The latter are always outsiders. The fact that someone on the state payroll runs their village upsets them deeply and throws a disturbing light on the reforms.

No matter how one adds up or balances out the various discrepancies described above, clearly the gap between 1978 earnings and 1986 earnings is not as great as the highly selective figures and dubious accounting procedures behind current reports suggest.

There remains another big reason why pre and postreform figures cannot be directly compared. The labor pool tapped in the two periods has not only significantly expanded, it has undergone qualitative change. In 1978 there were around 200 people in the village labor force. In 1986 there were more than 250, but the increase was not enough to staff all the enterprises. So the village went outside for help. Whereas prereform Dazhai employed little or no outside labor, postreform Dazhai now employs substantial numbers of nonresident laborers in its most profitable sideline, the coal mines, and probably elsewhere as well. One-third of the miners are from other villages— something like twenty-five out of seventy-five men. Thus the labor force has grown not only by fifty but by seventy-five and possibly more. Judging by trends elsewhere in China, one must assume that there are outside day laborers employed in Dazhai's other small plants, orchards, and on private trucks and tractors as well. The total increase, conservatively estimated, may well amount to a 40-percent rise in labor power since 1978.

This expanded labor force obviously swells the gross income of the village. It also expands the per capita income because even though outside workers take their wages home they leave behind the surplus value created by their labor. This component of gross income swells the accumulation fund owned by all residents and in the long run also pushes up per capita incomes realized as wages earned from new capital investments and as subsidized fringe benefits. One Shandong village that employs outside miners in a local gold mine is building 10,000-yuan houses for all its residents.

Third, while new enterprises have indeed brought in large amounts of added income, other prereform projects have declined or even collapsed. The truth is, if it were not for the coal mines, Dazhai income, corrected for inflation, could well be below that of 1978.

The starting date for all current reports is 1978. Dazhai gross income that year was 185,000 yuan. In 1983 the first coal mine came on stream, adding hundreds of thousands of yuan to the gross. By 1986 the coal produced sold for 350,000 yuan. Subtract this from the total income, given as 630,000 yuan, and you get 280,000 yuan from other sources. Cut this in half to correct for inflation and you have 140,000 yuan, 45,000 yuan below the gross figure for 1978. Even if the correction is exaggerated, the reform doesn't look all that good. How can this be?

It can be because the village abandoned several profitable collective enterprises after 1983 and at the same time failed to maintain the high standards of field and crop care that made Dazhai famous. The list of abandoned enterprises includes a bean noodle factory that earned 10,000 yuan and supplied by-product feed for a pig-raising project that earned 20,000; a blacksmith and welding shop that earned 7,000; a wine plant that earned 5,000; and a horse-raising project making use of rangeland elsewhere that earned 40,000 to 50,000. Altogether these projects produced 92,000 yuan worth of income that no longer comes in. The large building that once housed the bean noodle factory along with all its adjacent pigpens stands vacant on the slope of Tigerhead Mountain.

Other unused or underused resources on Tigerhead Mountain include many mulberry trees that once nourished silkworms and many walnut and persimmon trees that appear to be, if not abandoned, at least neglected.

Since the official line is that Dazhai, in the past, paid attention only to grain production, village leaders today introduce a number of still-functioning enterprises that were built long ago as if they were new, as if they were another result of the reform. These include the brick kiln which previously earned 20,000 yuan (Hinton family members worked there in 1971), the soysauce and vinegar plant which contributed 10,000, and several tractors which contributed 10,000, earned by hauling freight on the road.

Legitimate new enterprises, other than the coal mine, include a flour mill, a rock crusher, and additional privately owned trucks and tractors engaged in transportation. The new trucks and tractors bring in around 70,000 yuan, considerably less than the amount lost by closing down old enterprises.

Agriculture in Decline

The deterioration of agriculture since the reform is serious and plainly visible. With the exception of fruit from the expanding orchards, which Chinese class as a sideline, crop yields are falling. This year I saw only a few fields that had the kind of crops that made Dazhai famous in the days of Chen Yonggui—thick, dark green fast-growing luxuriant corn and sorghum. The plant growth standing in Dazhai fields this June reflected the wide range of management skills and commitment to farming that privatization has brought to the land. I noticed great variations in plant color, stalk height, seeding rates, germination rates, and crop care. I had to conclude that the contracting peasants of today are unlikely to match the collective crops of a decade ago, and the statistics bear this out.

The reformers like to dwell on the 1983 crop, the harvest collected during the first year of the reform. It was apparently bountiful, with an average yield of 149 bushels to the acre and a record total yield of 500 long tons of grain. The problem is that while this yield was often approached, even surpassed per acre, if not in total crop, in the past, it has not been duplicated since. The weather behaved ideally in 1983, and the soil, under collective care for decades, had reached a high state of fertility. Since then the weather has not been so favorable, and the contracting families have paid indifferent attention to fertility, seed quality, and other crucial inputs. Yields have suffered accordingly:

1984 .... 94 bushels per acre
1985 .... 105 bushels per acre
1986 (drought year).......... 94 bushels per acre
1987 (drought year).......... 35 bushels per acre (estimated)

Before the reform Dazhai also suffered drought years. 1982 was one of them. The reformers like to compare the 70 bushels per acre yield of that year with the bumper 149 bushel crop of 1983. However, in 1975 Dazhai, as a collective, harvested 129 bushels per acre; in 1976, 132 bushels per acre; in 1977, 154 bushels per acre; and in 1978, 113 bushels per acre. Even if these figures are exaggerated, as critics now claim, they cannot be reduced by much. I saw the crops in 1977 and 1978. They were the best I ever saw in Shanxi. To be fair, one should match good years against good years and bad years against bad years, not compare the worst with the best.

From the mid-1970s right through to the reform in the early 1980s the crops in Xiyang county, influenced by Dazhai's example, were excellent on the whole. At various times I saw them, admired them, and even marvelled that mountain terraces could produce so much. Since privatization in 1983 the trend has clearly been downhill, not only in Dazhai village but also in neighboring villages once known for their bountiful crops. Here, for example, are some figures for Shiping and Nannao:

Shiping

1973 .... 70 bu/acre (drought year)
1979 .... 103 bu/acre
1982 .... 47 bu/acre (drought year)
1986 .... 38 bu/acre (drought year)
1987 (estimated) less (drought year)

Nannao

1977 .... 110 bu/acre
1979 .... 99 bu/acre

1981	. . . .	57 bu/acre
1982	. . . .	57 bu/acre (drought year)
		year of reform
1986	. . . .	50 bu/acre (drought year)
1987	(estimated)	less (drought year)

Not only have yields decined in the last few years but the infrastructure, which includes terraces, access roads to fields, and irrigation systems, has deteriorated. At Dazhai the terraces seemed to be standing well. They are exceptionally well built. But the access road was eroding badly last June. An individual peasant had contracted the road-maintenance job and was clearly not living up to his contract. Over the county as a whole I saw many, many collapsed terraces, in some places as many as one quarter of the total. Each collapse means a reduction in crop area and a reduction in yield.

Random coal mining at Shiping has so disturbed the ground water that all the wells have run dry. If it were not for "West-Water-East," the local irrigation project so roundly denounced by the central government during the repudiation of Dazhai, the village would be without water.

Coal to the Rescue

As for Dazhai, with the abandonment of many old projects, declining yields on the land, and much of the infrastructure wearing out, all the reformers really can lay claim to are several new privately owned trucks and tractors running the road, a 25 percent expansion of fruit-orchard acreage, and two coal mines. However, since most of the fruit trees were planted long ago and are only now reaching bearing age, the reforms of 1983 hardly deserve credit. This leaves the question of the mines, by far the most important new source of income. All the trucks and tractors together only bring in 90,000 yuan, the orchards (old and new), 110,000. But the first mine shaft alone yields 350,000, making it the primary factor in the postreform economy. In 1987 coal production began at a second shaft which is supposed to yield more, in the long run, than the first. Coal mining will almost certainly dominate the Dazhai economy in the future.

But can the reformers legitimately claim credit for these mines? Are they something that would not exist without the reform? The answer, quite obviously, is no.

Dazhai, as a collective, went in for mining long ago. In the early 1960s under Chen Yonggui's leadership, work began on a coal pit. A bad accident held up the work. The village, preoccupied with capital construction on the land and reluctant to divert labor elsewhere gave up the effort for the time being. In the 1970s prospectors discovered bauxite in Xiyang county. Dazhai then opened a bauxite mine. Brigade members worked the ore successfully for several years, then abandoned the project when the market for local bauxite collapsed. Why the market collapsed is not clear to me, but it affected many mines in many villages. It was not something peculiar to Dazhai. According to reports made to me by Dazhai leaders in 1987, work began on the first new coal shaft in 1980, several years before the reform, but the mine came on stream in 1983, the year that the village parceled out the land. Coal began to flow just in time to give the reform a great boost. The peasants, however, began work on the mine while still organized as a collective. They created it as a community project, rooted in the collective tradition of the past and only contracted it out to an individual entrepreneur, one Liang Bingliang, when two years later they had privatized everything else. So how can the reform claim credit for the coal mine today?

Reformers may argue that under the collective system Dazhai could not hire miners from outside to work in the pit and thus could not mine on the scale that makes the mine profitable today. That may be true, but as a cooperative they could achieve the same scale by setting up a joint enterprise with one or more neighboring villages.

Reformers may argue that prior to 1979 the state claimed ownership over all mineral resources and discouraged local efforts to exploit them. This may also be true, yet long before 1979 many communes and villages in Xiyang county opened coal mines and bauxite mines, rock quarries, and lime pits. If state policy discouraged this, it was singularly ineffective. With the reform, state policy changed. It could have changed on this issue without any overall reform. The state did not have to carry out the privatization of farming in order to encourage, facilitate, and finance the collective exploitation of local resources.

Two contrasting experiences—failure to pursue coal mining in the 1960s and the success of Dazhai's mine today—are linked not so much to reform policy as to the history of off-farm resource development and infrastructural progress in Xiyang county as a whole. In the 1960s lots of coal lay underground in and around Yangquan City, the railroad town on the main trunk line from Shijiazhuang to Taiyuan. While the state opened huge mines there, supplying coal to burgeoning industries all over north and central China, the road south to Xiyang remained narrow, tortuous, and rough. High transportation costs discouraged aspiring miners in Xiyang's hills.

Today the situation is entirely different. Big units have all but mined out Yangquan coal. Buyers are looking for new sources of supply. The state has built a modern, hard-surface highway all the way into Xiyang and is now constructing a railroad to and through the town. Xiyang coal is both very much in demand and relatively easy to ship out. These favorable factors have done far more than reform policy, it seems to me, to induce Dazhai peasants to mine coal.

Behind the Defamation

One is impelled to ask: Why does the media in China so persistently distort the truth about Dazhai?

Deng and his group surged to power with the slogan "Seek Truth from Facts." Yet it seems that facts still carry little weight whenever they conflict with the demands of policy. Today's policy requires cadres to challenge Mao's model; better yet, overthrow it. Reports must show that the "responsibility system" works better than the collective system not only in some previously stagnant Sichuan or Anhui village, but above all right in Mao's chosen community in the Shanxi highlands.

Warping Dazhai's story in this way hardly squares with a serious commitment to "Seek Truth from Facts." Dazhai was a very successful example of "revolutionary politics in command," of "the socialist road," of "self-reliance in the main," and of "public first, self second" as the guiding principles of life. Dazhai owed its success, not to state subsidies and army manpower as the reformers now claim, but to the consistent hard work and cooperative spirit of Dazhai's citizens and to the genius of Chen Yonggui. If the cooperative movement had worked as well over China as a whole as it did at Dazhai, the whole question of rural reform would never have come up.

In the 1970s some 30 percent of China's villages, following the Dazhai model, were doing well. Another 40 percent, in the middle, showed potential but also confronted many problems. Thirty percent at the bottom, either misapplying or ignoring the Dazhai model, were stagnating. They were doing very poorly indeed. The responsibility system arose as an answer for that bottom 30 percent. Applied there, it quickly solved many problems. The party and government then spread it to the whole country, fanning up a reform wind that swept all of the intermediate villages and finally most of the leading villages along the same path regardless of the wishes of the inhabitants. To clear the way, to make privatization irresistible, the reformers evidently felt they had to discredit, undermine, and transform all leading examples of the collective period, either that or ignore them, by-pass them, and leave them in political, social, and economic limbo. This latter method worked with communities that were not very well known, but it would hardly do for famous brigades like Dazhai or Long Bow. Thus the bizarre contradiction between the slogan "Seek Truth from Facts" and the practice of the reform whenever it came face to face with a thriving, well-known cooperative village. Truth, as had so often been the case in prior periods of upheaval and change in China, became the first casualty of the reform.

Truth has long been a casualty on the wage-labor front. Having defined socialism as "public ownership" plus "distribution according to work performed," reform leaders have consistently denied that some peasants were hiring others and getting rich by expropriating the surplus value thus generated. By the same token they have long ignored the kind of productive relations set up since the reform at the coal mines in Dazhai, whereby one community expropriates the surplus value created by the labor force of another. Such arrangements raise serious problems for the transition to socialism and should be high on the agenda in any discussion of the future of Chinese society. Yet month after month, year after year, official spokesmen for rural policy have reiterated only the oft-heard proposition that it is perfectly all right for some people to get rich first since they are getting rich by working hard. Others need only apply themselves to catch up.

Now finally, at the Thirteenth Party Congress, China's leaders have done an about-face. Henceforth, the documents state, no limits will be placed on the hiring of wage labor whether by individuals, stock companies, or cooperative communities. The practice is a legitimate one at the current stage of development. All this is given theoretical justification by the sudden creation of a new stage of socialism—"the primary stage"—and of a new category of enterprises—"private" as distinct from "individual." This latter term now turns out to refer only to self-employed craftsmen and "mom-and-pop" store-type ventures which can graduate to "private" status as the number of employees grows.

This is refreshing. No more denials, no more evasions, just open support for the kind of primitive accumulation through exploitation of wage labor that has been spreading across the country for a long time.

But the implications for socialism are no less serious than they were before the admission. Justifying anything and everything that promotes the development of productive forces on the grounds that this is the primary stage of socialism is neither adequate as theory nor reassuring as practice. Mixed economies are inherently unstable. That's why Mao pushed cooperation in the first place. It is by no means self-evident that public ownership of land, resources, and major productive equipment will lead to socialism under a system where the bulk of these resources are contracted out to individuals with full managerial privileges, including the right to hire and fire, buy and sell, build up or liquidate. What is emerging side-by-side with a rapidly expanding private sector of the economy is a universal, multilayered concession system that lavishly rewards those who control productive resources, and most lavishly rewards those who control the most.

Under these new arrangements all sectors of the economy generate social polarization on a massive scale and simultaneously build up vested interests in a reform status quo that tilts precariously toward capitalism—all this at a time when capitalism, on a world scale, is entering upon unprecedented crisis.

Since the reforms carried out in 1983, polarization has been no stranger to Dazhai. While those who contract enterprises or purchase trucks and tractors with cheap government credit can parlay their control over means of production into family incomes in excess of 10,000 yuan per year, others who lack labor power, capital or credit have sunk to bare subsistence levels. A former women's leader tills three mu (all she can handle). She sold 600 jin of grain in 1986 for 100 yuan and in addition received a pension of 72 yuan for herself and 72 yuan for her aging husband. However, she never saw a substantial part of this pension money. The township checked it off as payment on the color TV which she now owns but in which she enjoys little equity. While boasting of the number of TVs and appliances owned by Dazhai citizens, the newspapers fail to tell how many are actually paid for.

So what used to be a community of relatively equal laboring people who shared their collective income on the basis of work performed is rapidly turning into a stratified community consisting of a well-to-do minority moving into position to realize unearned incomes, a middle income majority (many of them primarily wage workers), and a substrata of the poor, handicapped primarily by the lack of labor power. Capital assets including means of production held or controlled now have more to do with income levels than work done.

Ironic Lessons, Past and Present

In summing up the lessons of Dazhai, past and present, one can hardly avoid being overwhelmed by the irony of its current situation. The village that was once China's primary symbol of cooperation has now turned into its opposite. Today's Dazhai can easily stand as a symbol of the pitfalls that, with the maturing of reform, confront all agriculture. While new policies have undoubtedly stimulated a considerable upsurge in rural sideline production, particularly in areas such as Xiyang county where there are nonfarm resources like coal, it is increasingly clear that on the land, in crop production and especially in grain production, the reforms lack "staying power." Following a year of peak production in 1984, grain output dropped back 30 million tons in 1985 and has virtually stagnated since. Many signs indicate that the 1987 crop, not yet reported, may well be sharply down.[2]

The *China Daily* of October 31, 1987, quotes Deng Xiaoping as saying he expects development in all other fields to go well during all of the 1990s but that he is deeply concerned about agricultural production. Other leaders recently quoted in the same paper complain about

---

2. The latest claim (*China Daily*, February 2, 1988), is a grain output of 401.2 million tons in 1987. But this figure is suspect. It is almost exactly the figure that the plan called for. Chinese officials, when making up annual reports and given a choice between planned figures and real ones, will almost always report the plan as an accomplishment. Who wants to rock the boat by taking responsibility for anything else?

the negative results of the reform—the damage done to water conservancy projects, the shrinking area of cultivated land, the drop in soil fertility, the lowered resistance of soils to disaster, and the weakening of institutions that provide technical services to rural people. The *China Daily* reports that the root cause of all these problems is "the imperfect mechanism for rural accumulation fund. . . . We used to think that farmers would tackle the problem of expanding production by themselves . . . but we failed to see how much ability farmers have for accumulation. . . . Farmers in recent years have used their income mainly for nonproductive purposes, such as buying consumer goods and building houses."

Dazhai today vividly illustrates every one of these problems. While nonfarm enterprises—coal mines, trucks, tractors for transport—flourish, agriculture slowly declines, infrastructure washes out, fertility drops, yields fall, technical support fades. Most shocking is the realization that Dazhai, the village that once sold a higher proportion of its crop to the state than the big mechanized state farms on the virgin lands of the northeast, this year (according to figures given to us) raised too little grain to feed its own population.

In 1987 the village planted 83.3 acres of corn that yielded an estimated 35 bushels per acre for a total of over 2,900 bushels. Since no one eats corn any more, Dazhai peasants swap the corn for wheat at the rate of two pounds of corn to one pound of wheat flour. 2,900 bushels of corn amounts to 82 tons of dry shelled corn which can be swapped for 41 tons of wheat flour. Since, on the average, each person consumes 0.7 lbs of wheat flour a day, the 504 people of Dazhai consume 128,772 pounds a year, or a little more than 64 tons. Thus, according to official figures, they are 23 tons short in 1987. Will they go hungry? No. Because every year they under-report the crop, hold grain in reserve, and have something to tide them over a bad year. This year many families are still eating grain left over from the bumper crop of 1983.

That being the case, how does the government know how much grain is harvested each year? The answer is the government doesn't know. Nobody knows. What *is* known, nevertheless, is that crops are getting smaller. To Dazhai people it doesn't matter. Almost every family has members engaged in sideline production. In the mines people make 9 yuan a day. Grain that miners don't raise they can buy. But if these declining yields are extrapolated out to cover the country as a whole, the gravity of the situation becomes obvious.

If too many villages fail to raise enough grain to feed themselves, the shortages will eventually reach a point where they cannot be made up from any alternative source. That is the spectre that haunts the reform-ers. That is the soft underbelly of the responsibility system. In China grain production is no sideline. It is, as Mao so often said, the key link. When you are concerned, as Deng is, about agricultural production and especially grain production in the 1990s, you are concerned about the main activity, the bedrock livelihood, of some 800,000,000 people, and about food supplies for over 1 billion. You are concerned about the heart of the economy. On this front the peasants of China have yet to be heard from. So far they have been voting with their feet.

大 Mao's
回 Rural Policies
潮 Revisited

A question raised by the agricultural reforms in China is: Did collective failures, overall, outnumber collective successes? My conclusion is that they did not. A group of young economists who did the analysis that led up to the reforms told me in 1980 that some 30 percent of the village collectives were doing well, another 30 percent were doing very poorly, and in the middle the remaining 40 percent could be said to be neither thriving nor collapsing, but that nevertheless they confronted many problems. Given this information one could make various statements. One could add the bottom 30 percent and the middle 40 percent together and say that the majority were doing poorly. One could add the top 30 percent and the middle 40 percent and say that the majority were at least viable. Or one could say that the successes and the failures were about equal (top and bottom 40 percent), while mixed results predominated (middle 40 percent).

I think the last of these is the most realistic. Furthermore, I think that a cooperative movement that is 30 percent successful is an extraordinary achievement in a country the size of China. That means that some 240 million people have done well as cooperators. If this many people could do well working together cooperation was certainly

---

After "Dazhai Revisited" appeared in *Monthly Review* (March 1988), Hugh Deane wrote a response, both to that article and the correspondence piece by Herb and Ruth Gansberg, "More on Dazhai" (September 1988). His article represents an apt summary of the "reformers'" case against Mao's policies in general and his rural policies in particular, and the present article was accordingly written to reply to this case, focusing on its major points.

a viable way of life for Chinese peasants. The 240 million peasants who were doing badly could, with government help, reorganization, and hard work, also learn to do well. The same applies to those 320 million who were cooperating with mixed results in the middle of the spectrum.

Of course, my informants may have had the ratios wrong. If there are other surveys that come up with some different proportions for failures and successes they should be laid on the table. But even if the successful coops made up a significantly smaller proportion of the whole, if tens of millions of peasants learned to prosper cooperatively, the implications are extraordinary, because what millions can do, other millions can also do. That's why the question of whether Dazhai, heralded throughout the country in Mao's day as a successful model, is so important. If Dazhai was a success Dazhai showed a road forward that other peasants could follow.

The Grain Front

I do not dispute the conclusion that during the collective period China's grain production just barely kept pace with population growth. This was true in spite of the fact that many well-run collectives doubled, tripled, and quadrupled their output. It follows that large numbers of collectives never realized their potential but it does not follow that the cooperative organization of agriculture is, by nature, unworkable. Since it has been replaced for at least five or six years now by a production system based on family contracts it is in order to ask, has the new system done any better with per capita grain production?

The answer is, apparently not. Since 1984, when the government reported grain production at over 400 million tons, the official figures record a sharp slump, then a slow rise that has not managed to recoup the ground lost in 1985. Now the press routinely talks of stagnation in grain production, of grain shortages, of falling production, and this year finally of 20 million peasants faced with famine, 80 million in serious straits and 200 million with short crops.

Moreover, to the best of my knowledge China never produced the 400 million tons it now claims to have produced in 1984. The ample supply of market grain that year came only in part from current production. Released stocks of collective grain supplied the surplus. This grain was sold on the market or distributed to peasants when the collectives broke up. Sellers were able to market it to great advantage due to the sharp increase in grain prices that accompanied the reform and to the bonuses paid for above quota grain. By the same token the big tonnage drop reported in 1985 was not due primarily to production failures, but to the exhaustion of stored grain. The real crop harvested annually from 1983 to 1988 has hovered between 350 million and 380 million tons. If we take the higher figure (which is pretty optimistic), and allocate it among 1.1 billion people (currently estimated population), we come up with an average of 345 kg. of grain per person, which is not very much higher than the average in 1978 as reported by Hugh Deane. The reform, it seems, has not broken the back of the grain problem.

This is not to say that all directives and policies concerning collectivization were correct. A point frequently raised by the reformers is that in the collective period, exaggerated implementation of Mao's "grain is the key link" policy seriously limited rural diversification. It seems clear that during the cooperative period the government, at times, put too much stress on grain to the detriment of oil and industrial crops and specialties such as fruit, livestock, and sidelines. What is not at all clear is the reason for this and who should be held responsible. There was nothing wrong with Mao's slogan. It was well rounded and went, "Take grain as the key link, practice animal husbandry, forestry, fisheries, and side occupations to create all around rural prosperity." That slogan was good then and it is good now. The very designation of grain as a "link" means that grain is not "all" and that other links in the chain must and can be developed as long as grain production is handled well.

If, during certain periods, one-sided policies reduced diversification, then the solution is to correct those one-sided policies. There is nothing about the cooperative movement as such that inhibits diversification. In fact, well-led cooperatives are in a much better position to diversify, to use all skills, all talents, and all resources, than individual peasants in a privatized economy. Many outstanding communities demonstrated this over and over again, in the 1960s, 1970s, and 1980s. One recent example is Doudian village in the Beijing suburbs today.

Another point Deane raises, again echoing the reformers, is that living conditions stagnated in the cooperative period. And it is true, over wide areas, where cooperatives were not doing well, living standards did stagnate. In other areas they did not. Certain communities developed remarkable prosperity. The figure of 42.8 percent of the brigades with a per capita income below 50 yuan a year seems to contradict the figures given to me about the 30-40-30 split. But it's not clear what this figure refers to, whether it is total income or disposable income. In the cooperative period many services and benefits were distributed free of charge. People also earned a share of their coop's accumulation fund and were enriched as owners by their coop's investments. Production expenses were all paid by the community. Before comparisons are made the concepts being compared must be analyzed with care. Real incomes were probably at least double the 50 yuan reported. But of course, in terms of daily satisfaction, a larger disposable income is a necessity and the countryside as a whole did not advance as it should have, as it had the potential to do, in the 1960s and 1970s. Stagnant areas, whether 30 percent or 42.8 percent, were far too numerous and far too extensive. The countryside demanded change. The issue is not whether there should have been change, but what that change should be. Were there no effective options available within the context of the cooperative system that could overcome stagnation? Was privatization the preferred solution to the problems that arose?

Another charge is that rural impoverishment was particulary severe in the rural Northwest. Remote upland areas did tend to lag behind after liberation, despite some special attention given to them from Beijing. The land is poor, markets far away, nonagricultural opportunities meager. These problems confronted peasant coops and they still confront individual peasant contractors today. Only today peasants face them alone, family by family, in a one-on-one battle against nature and the impartial market, instead of together as a community. Depending on how well or how badly a given coop was managed, historically this might be an advantage or a disadvantage, but on the whole a peasant in the loess highlands will find it difficult to face life alone.

I spent a month in the loess highlands northeast of Yenan in 1988. My impression was that the situation was pretty desperate. Contracted crop fields could not provide sufficient food because, for one thing, the peasants could not afford fertilizer, or even get it if they could afford it.

As a result, they were tilling the mountain slopes as "help-out land" and destroying them in the process. Dams, terraces, and other collective engineering works were falling apart. We saw abandoned irrigation systems and washed-out earthworks. It was quite clear that many of them never would have been built under a private economy and that they would not now be restored short of recollectivization. Peasants we talked to at random were angry and said they were better off under the coop system.

The Price Scissors

One very serious charge, brought up by Deane, is that Mao's socialist policies squeezed excessive surplus out of the peasants. China was and is primarily an agricultural country. Accumulation for industrial investment had to come out of agriculture to start with. There was no other choice. The new government did indeed set the purchase price for grain and other agricultural products low. These low prices made it possible to supply the cities with low-priced food and thus to keep urban workers wages low as well. This policy also provided raw materials at low prices. With cheap food and raw materials accumulation rates in industry were high. However, some of this accumulation went back into agricultural inputs such as machinery, equipment, fertilizer, and pesticides. From 1953 to 1977 4.27 percent of total investment in industry went toward agricultural input, and these inputs were sold back to peasant coops at very low prices, prices that fell as time went on. In 1959 peasants had to come up with 116,500 kg. of wheat to buy a 75-horsepower track tractor. By 1979 this fell to 53,500 kg. In 1950 it took 1.6 kg. of wheat to buy 1 kg. of fertilizer. By 1979, 0.5 kg. of wheat would buy 1. kg. of fertilizer. In 1960, it took 35 kg. of wheat to buy 1 kg. of pesticide. By 1979, this had decreased to 5 kg.[1]

The agricultural sector was exploited but it was not drained. On the contrary, it was continuously replenished with modern products through a mutually supportive relationship that reduced the overall depletion of the countryside and mitigated the effect of the classical "scissors," (the discrepancy between agricultural and industrial prices).

---

1. Figures reported by Ching Pao-yu, *"China's Rural Reform and Grain,"* unpub. ms., November 1988.

Furthermore, the state helped rural areas with direct investment in agricultural infrastructure. This increased from 7.3 percent of total investment in the first five-year plan to 11.4 percent in 1978 (the fifth five-year plan period). The ratio of state investment in agriculture to direct receipts from agriculture went from 49 percent in the first five-year plan period to 56 percent in the second period, to 164 percent in the fourth and fifth periods.[2]

Since 1980, both direct state investment in agriculture and state investment in industries providing agricultural inputs have fallen away sharply. Investment in industries supplying inputs dropped from the 1953–1977 average of 4.27 percent to a 1980–1985 average of 1.3 percent. Meanwhile, direct investment in infrastructure fell from a high of 11.5 percent in 1978 to 6.3 percent in the period 1980–1985, and then down to 4 percent in the period 1985–1987. At the same time the peasants' own investment of labor in capital construction (primarily agricultural infrastructure) fell from as high as 8 billion work days per year in the late 1970s to less than a quarter of that today. These two reductions combined (reduced state funds and reduced peasant labor input) amount to a critical, one might say ruinous, retreat from the transformation of nature, from the Dazhai-inspired effort to achieve high, stable yields through conservation engineering.[3]

Meanwhile, in spite of substantial price increases for grain and other agricultural products, the classical "scissors" has opened wide. In the last five to seven years fertilizer prices have gone up 37.7 percent to 60 percent, diesel fuel up 22 percent, electricity up 167 percent and irrigation water up 100 percent to 200 percent, bringing in their wake substantial increases in the cost of production and substantial decreases in the amount of cash actually spent by peasants for industrial inputs, which translated into even more radical decreases in the amount of these inputs actually purchased.[4] It goes without saying, I think, that the more broadly peasant producers enter the market, the more severe the impact of the "scissors" will be, and the more heavily they will be exploited.

Deane also maintains that Mao's policies resulted in excessive accumulation rates. Yes, I think they sometimes did. In their enthusiasm

---

2. Ibid.
3. Ibid.
4. Ibid.

to transform the world quickly, misguided cadre did push accumulation rates to irrational levels during certain periods and in certain places. Whether this was true overall for the whole countryside is not clear. I guess a pretty good case could be made. However, this is not a factor built into cooperation as a system. Accumulation rates are determined by policy, rates that are too high can be adjusted. One need not abandon the whole system to achieve a reasonable balance between consumption and investment.

Deane's statement that the proportion of accumulation funds spent on welfare dropped from 40.2 percent to 22.5 percent in two decades needs further analysis. These figures do not necessarily mean any absolute drop in welfare funds. It all depends on the size of the accumulation funds. Since production did go up, albeit too slowly, accumulation also presumably went up.

The Problem of Commandism

Reformers now argue that Mao's impetuosity forced peasants into coops by command before they were ready, thus doing serious damage to the cooperative movement and agricultural production. To be sure, commandism was widespread not only during the period of the formation of coops but throughout the collective period. Cadres rushed many peasants into cooperation before they were ready for it, before the form had proved its worth to them. This violated the spirit of voluntarism and seriously maimed the movement in many places. Coops set up by command tended to degenerate into stagnant feudal fiefs, run by local Communist lords who were, in some cases, as bad if not worse than the landlords they replaced.

Commandism, in the form of bureaucratic intervention in the day-to-day operation of even the best of coops, also held back their development. Coops badly needed more autonomy overall and especially more autonomy in the management of their resources and the allocation of their investments. I think it is fair to say that if coops had been granted half the autonomy that individuals were automatically granted once they contracted the land in the 1980s a far larger proportion of coops would have done well. One provision of the new regulations alone introduced great flexibility into the system. This was the provision that peasants did not have to grow the grain they contracted to deliver. They could grow some other crop, sell it, and buy enough grain to fulfill their quota. Thus each producer could decide, at the grassroots, what crops made most sense, what crops yielded the greatest return. Cooperative units could have been granted considerable autonomy on this question and then, if grain production suffered, the government could have used price incentives to restore the balance as they have done again and again since the reform. Recently the manipulation of prices has led to serious imbalances, but that is a separate question arising from the way in which the market has been manipulated and linked to reneging on price promises, uncontrolled inflation in the prices of farm inputs, corruption, and many other factors relating to the new situation created by the reform.

No question, commandism has been a serious and continuing problem, but it is difficult to argue that commandism and cooperation go together. The solution to command problems is surely to introduce more autonomy, more democracy, into the system and to use market mechanisms rather than government directives to influence production decisions. There is no reason why tens of thousands of cooperative units can't relate to each other and to the state-operated economy through the market just as individuals now do. The commandism that so damaged the cooperative movement was in great measure simply an extension of the bureaucratic centralism of the past cranked up several notches and reinvigorated by the centralist tradition of the Communist movement. Functionaries in China just assume that they have a right to run everything, down to the smallest details of people's lives. This tradition is really feudal. It is deeply resented down below and that is one of the reasons for the extraordinary attraction that a free market economy such as the one now appearing in Shenjen has for ordinary Chinese citizens. For people suffering under feudal restraints the cash nexus seems to promise a radical liberation where ability and not influence derived from social connections count. (So far, of course it is the high cadres' children who have been able to get their hands on the cash and dominate the nexus.)

The irony built into this commandism question is that the reformers, under an anticommand banner, dismantled the rural cooperative economy by command. Certainly many peasants welcomed the family contract system and voted with their feet to abandon cooperatives, but many other peasants did not. Deane would have to back up the statement he makes about peasants voting with their feet to abandon the collectives with some believable data before that question can be settled. Changing direction with "one stroke of the knife" (complete, all-out change without any room for compromise or divergence) is notoriously prevalent in China. Cadres at all levels, mobilized from the center, fan strong political winds and impose heavy sanctions on foot dragging, not to mention opposition or obstruction. So it is very difficult to know what people really think or really want. Just as commandism rushed many unwilling peasants into collectives in the first place, so commandism rushed many unwilling peasants out of them in the second place.

The Privatization Wind

Long Bow village resisted family contracts for two years and yielded in the end only because higher Communist Party leaders confronted the local party committee with an ultimatum: contract the land within one month or face expulsion from the party. Wanggongzhuang leaders avoided such an ultimatum by disappearing whenever county leaders came to initiate reform.

Scattered throughout China one finds communities that either didn't change their collective system at all or made only surface changes to comply with government directives while maintaining a strong collective core. Unfortunately, from my point of view, they make up only a small fraction of the total, probably less than 1 percent, which calls into question the conclusion that they are still in contention. The problem here is to get any realistic picture of the wishes of the peasantry. Given the scale of the campaign, given the penalties for noncompliance, given the very substantial rewards for compliance, and realizing that it is always easier to return to the past than to pioneer the future, it is not surprising that the reformers were able to dissolve coops wholesale even where they were doing well.

There is no question that over large areas where the rural economy was stagnating, where collectives represented something much closer to feudal fiefs tilled by serfs than to voluntary communities of enfranchised producers, peasants celebrated the reforms as a "Second Liberation." They were absolutely delighted to get the cadres off their backs. But in the country as a whole, peasants found themselves in a variety of situations that included regions where large numbers of successful coops existed side by side with even larger numbers of less successful ones where the prospects were mixed, all interspersed with certain communities where the prospects were dismal.

The response of individual families in each of these situations could differ sharply. Even in the best managed, most successful coops, loyally supported by most of their members, ambitious individuals with special skills and labor power dreamed of going it alone. The less successful the coop, the more prevalent such attitudes. At the same time, even in poorly managed coops, there were many families who had no special skills, who had little or no ablebodied labor, who looked on cooperation as their salvation, hence wanted to continue the coops. And here and there, throughout the system, scattered in the most unlikely places, one found individuals with extraordinary talents who could prosper in any situation but who, inspired by socialist ideals, saw cooperation as *the* way out for the Chinese peasantry as a whole and devoted their lives to making it work. They asked no more for themselves than an equal share in the common prosperity to come. I have personally known quite a few such people. Reform-minded cadres have attacked them as "conservatives" who oppose privatization because it jeopardizes their status as coop cadres.

Most people either do not know or simply ignore the extent to which, in the course of the reform, state decrees warped law, regulations, fiscal, and monetary policy in support of private production and against cooperation. Central Document No. 1 for 1983 legalized the private hiring of labor, the private purchase of large-scale producer goods (processing equipment, tractors, trucks), the pooling of capital for private investment, and the leasing of collective property to individuals. In the wake of all this, individuals also began privately loaning out money at usurious rates. The new fiscal and credit policy gave tax holidays to new private businesses and authorized liberal bank loans to such businesses as well as to specialized single households, while at the same time virtually cutting off credit to the existing producers cooperatives, the village brigades. The larger the enterprise operated by the specialized household, the larger the private business, the better the terms of the loan, and the easier it became to get one. Private contractors who leased collective enterprises had the right to hire and fire, set wage levels and profit margins, and, if they reinvested heavily in the enterprise, the right to gradually convert the whole thing into private property.

Most people, furthermore, do not know about, or simply ignore, the scandalous rip-off that dominated the liquidation of collective property and helped create those so-called specialized families with the requisite "money, strength, and ability" to get rich first. When the time came to distribute collective assets, people with influence and connections—cadres, their relatives, friends, and cronies—were able to buy, at massive discounts, the tractors, trucks, wells, pumps, processing equipment, and other productive property that the collectives had accumulated over decades through the hard labor of all members. Not only did the buyers manage to set low prices for these capital assets (often one third or less of their true value) but they often bought them with easy credit from state banks and then in the end, often failed to pay what they had promised. It is doubtful if, in the history of the world, any privileged group ever acquired more for less. The scale of these transactions and the depth of the injury done to the average coop member boggles the mind.

Given the rapid liquidation of public assets, the wholesale enrichment of those among the privileged who had the presence of mind to put their lips to the trough in time, and the preferential treatment granted thereafter to everyone with enough wealth to become a "specialist," it is not surprising that the reform had a snowball effect, capable of carrying whole regions before it. Once such an "enrich yourself wind" starts to blow it does not take long for most people to realize that the devil will take the hindmost and they had better jump in while the getting is good. To stand fast, to hold a good coop together because of its long-range advantages, is extremely difficult when all around you are grabbing at immediate wealth and advantage. And not only that, the peasants of privatized communities had a tendency to regard the crops and property of still-existing collectives as ripe for the taking, just one more pool of public property waiting to be liquidated. Collectives thus turned into besieged islands, very difficult to defend and very hard to hold together.

Mindful of the above circumstances, it is almost irrelevant to ask what proportion of the peasants supported the reforms. The choice that confronted them when the time came was not one between two systems. They had already been decided at the central level. What peasant heads of household had to decide was how to maximize family holdings and family incomes as their cooperatives broke up, how to get the most while the getting was good so as not to be at a disadvantage in the future.

The claim often made, and which Deane makes again, that labor productivity declined during the Mao era and rose sharply in the reform era, is questionable. While it is true that in poorly run coops people put in a lot of unproductive hours because morale was low, at the same time the very scale of production, the large size of the fields, the rational layout of irrigation channels, the use of field machinery—if only for plowing and harrowing—offset, to a certain extent, the problems of motivation. In the first flush of reform significantly fewer people farmed the same amount of land as before and raised yields on it but they did it with an enormous increase in labor expended. While unit yields (yields per acre) may have gone up, labor productivity in terms of bushels of crops grown per hour expended almost certainly went down. The main reason for this is the fractured fields. Reform split large fields into narrow strips, often not more than a few yards or a few feet wide. In many cases contracting peasants could not even get carts into the fields to unload manure or load crops, not to mention manage to plow, plant, or harvest with tractors. The reform confirmed the hoe as the preeminent farm implement and ensured that it would not soon be superseded by anything more modern.

Viewed realistically, the reform generated a massive speedup. People got up earlier, worked harder, stayed in the fields longer to create by intensive hand labor on miniscule strips what could have been, given any adequate scale, rationalized and modernized step by step. The figures concerning the rapid increase in tractors in recent years do not contradict this, since most of the tractors are never used on the land anyway; they are used for transport to and from fields and out on the highway. To the extent that tractors are used in the fields there is a problem of redundancy due to the small size of the holdings. In order to farm at all, peasants must have a certain set of implements and equipment. But, given the small scale and scattered nature of their contracted plots, they have little choice but to overinvest.

Deane also reiterates the conclusion that not only was the Great

Leap Forward a disaster, but that Mao should take sole blame for it. How should the Great Leap be appraised? There is general agreement, I think, that utopianism, voluntarism, commandism, gigantism, egalitarianism, exaggeration winds, and other ills all marred the Great Leap, that they generated chaos in the economy and in social life and contributed heavily to production crises, crop failures, and finally famine. (How extensive and damaging the famine was is still not clear.) At this late date it is fruitless to argue over the relative weight of bad weather versus bad politics in bringing on the debacle. Both played major roles. It makes some sense, however, to look into the question of Great Leap politics more deeply and to ask whether Mao's vision was itself fundamentally flawed or whether it was irreparably warped in the execution, and if so how this came about.

The overall strategy of the Great Leap was to mobilize China's vast idle, rural labor reserve to tap some of the country's enormous unused resources—marginal lands, irrigation waters, fossil fuels, and minerals. Not an unreasonable goal. In the course of the drive, Hunan peasants created some communes as a means for concentrating labor for big projects. Mao approved. He saw them as a way to unleash human potential and set the stage for continuing revolution. Through the creation of new, nonbureaucratic, self-governing institutions that combined industry, agriculture, commerce, education, and military affairs in one autonomous local unit, the peasants had taken a step toward supplanting traditional state power.

All this alarmed certain forces in the party, forces that had opposed agricultural producers cooperatives as "erroneous, dangerous and Utopian." These leaders had even less use for communes. Maurice Meisner writes:

> The political functions which Maoists assigned to the communes in theory, and the realities of communization, posed a grave challenge to the existing party and state bureaucracies. Had the people's communes actually developed in the manner Maoists originally envisaged, centralized political power in China would have been fundamentally undermined— much in the way in which Marx had attributed to the Paris Commune the potential to restore to the producers those social powers which had been usurped by the state. The antibureaucratic implications of communization were unmistakable, and bureaucrats with vested interests in the pre-Great Leap order soon began to respond to the threat.[5]

5. Maurice Meisner, *Mao's China* (New York: The Free Press, 1977), p. 241.

This passage points up a matter that tends to be slighted by conventional academic wisdom and by current Chinese accounts—that is, the political context of the times, the fundamental split within the Communist Party and in Chinese society generally over the direction of the revolution after the Communists won power.

After 1949 two headquarters, long latent in the party, crystalized out. One, headed by Mao, advocated building socialism as soon as land reform was completed. The other, headed by Liu Shaoch'i and Deng Xiaoping, favored an indefinite extension for and consolidation of the mixed economy of New Democracy (now called the primary stage of socialism by reformers). Each side had adherents at the very top and roots in the middle and lower levels of the party as well as in society. Since Liu's group controlled the Party Organization Department, responsible for recruiting, discipline, education, and party building in general, it could be argued that they had more clout in the day-to-day formulation and administration of policy. Nevertheless, on the question of agricultural cooperation Mao carried the day. What transpired in real life, however, was not the straightforward mobilization of the peasantry to build cooperatives, but a severe and protracted tug-of-war, a succession of actions and reactions, initiatives and counterinitiatives, generated by the opposing sides. The struggle started with the first faltering steps toward mutual aid and ran right through to the emergence of communes and beyond. It continues to this day, even though the vast majority of rural collectives have long since disbanded.

The predominance of Mao was never more than marginal. It depended in great measure on his ability to elicit support from below. He often bypassed the opposition by speaking directly to activists and ordinary people at the grass roots. He thus presented Liu and Deng with a series of *faits accomplis,* which they in turn responded to with *faits accomplis* of their own, the latter carried out by the wide network of functionaries under their organizational control.

Under these circumstances policies tended to suffer severe warp, sometimes to the point of a caricature or even mirror image of the original, their effectiveness gutted, their shortcomings magnified. One could hardly expect functionaries who had little trust in the outcome or opposed the whole concept to carry out such complex matters as coop and commune building in good faith. They were sensitive to various negative signals from the Central Committee. They knew how to drag their feet, how to carry out low-profile opposition, or even how to jump in and carry official directives to absurd lengths, thus assuring that initiatives would fall of their own weight.

Conventional wisdom now attributes to Mao and Maoists everything extreme, ultra left, Utopian, and voluntarist, while crediting Liu and his group with a consistent, sober, mixed economy line. While it seems clear that Mao did overestimate the socialist enthusiasm of the masses and opened the door to extremism with talk of a "transition to communism," his position was not nearly as "left" as is currently painted. For example, he projected twenty, not two, five year plans (100 years, not 10) for the transition from collective to communist ownership, and categorically opposed collective usurpation of private property and other forms of "leveling" rampant in those days.

Left in Form, Right in Essence

On the other side of the coin, there is much evidence to show that Liu, over a long period of time, repeatedly swung from right opportunism, even capitulation, to "left" adventurism on major policy issues. Confronted with the specter of a post-World War II civil war, he backed away from land reform, but once land reform broke out and could no longer be denied, he jumped in and pushed it far to the "left" with a "poor and hired peasants line," an extreme egalitarian program that almost brought the revolution to disaster by alienating the middle peasants and all other middle forces. This line targeted for attack the great mass of peasant activists who actually carried through the land reform because they had failed to create "equality," a destructive ultraleft initiative that failed to distinguish clearly between friends and enemies. In the Socialist Education Movement, and later during the Cultural Revolution, Liu came forward with "left in form, right in essence" lines that, under superrevolutionary rhetoric, repeatedly targeted the mass of cadres down below rather than expose the misleaders up above. This helped derail Mao's campaign against "party people in authority taking the capitalist road."

While it is hard to prove that Liu's cohorts consciously used ultraleft tactics during the Great Leap period, many of the extreme actions that threw the countryside into chaos at the time bear the by now familiar "left in form, right in essence" flavor so characteristic of Liu's counterthrusts over the years. All of them made use of "one stroke of the knife" technique. When a policy comes down, seize on one aspect of it and ride it into the ground. If Mao calls for taking grain as the key link take grain as *all*, rip out orchards to plant grain, cut back on oil seed crops to plant grain, plant grain on slopes that should grow trees, and so on. If Mao calls for deep tillage, start digging one foot deep, then two, then three, thus wasting countless labor days. And the same goes for close planting, backyard iron and steel production, free supply, community kitchens, the militarization of rural labor—carry everything to extremes. Since a large part of the bureaucracy, especially at the middle level, was made up of Liu-recruited and Liu-controlled cadres, it is hard to blame Maoists alone for all these follies. Provocation has long been an important weapon in the arsenal of China's mandarins. There is no better way to discredit an action than to carry it to absurd lengths. Would it not make sense for these forces, once they failed to stop any movement, to jump in and steer it toward disastrous ends? If you can't lick 'em join 'em. Turn predictions of disaster into a self-fulfilling prophecy. I believe such actions did occur.

From a different perspective, all the above arguments are irrelevant as regards the main point under discussion: the viability of agricultural producer's cooperatives as a basis for the rural economy of China. If the movement went off the track with extremes in 1958 what eventually crystalized out was a three-tiered team-brigade-commune system that worked well for hundreds of millions of peasants through the mid 1960s, the whole of the 1970s, and into the 1980s. To condemn it for detours taken and disasters generated years before, makes little sense. Cooperatives should be judged on their accomplishments, which were considerable, and on their potential, which was enormous, since they provided the scale and the infrastructure for the modernization and mechanization of the Chinese countryside, a development that has been severely hampered if not totally aborted by the family-contract system.

Deane brings up another issue, the question of environmental damage done by water conservancy projects during the Great Leap. In particular he mentions the salinization and alkalization of sections of the North China plain. Undoubtedly some of the Great Leap projects did damage the environment in certain localities. However, the damage done at that time was more than balanced out by projects which protected the environment. Furthermore, any damage caused by the Great Leap pales to insignificance compared to the wholesale attack on the environment in almost all regions of China since the implementation of the responsibility system. Since the slogans now are "some must get rich first," "to get rich is glorious," and "enrich yourselves," hundreds of millions of peasants are doing whatever helps them in the short term to increase income. Herdsmen have stepped up overgrazing in the grasslands, while farmers have stepped up plowing there, foresters and timber-hungry peasants have recklessly cut timber wherever they can find it. Everywhere and particularly in the loess highlands of North Shanxi, the mountainous regions of western Sichuan, and the mountains of North Hobei (areas I have personally observed), peasants are opening up mountain slopes that never should be cultivated, and doing it on a massive scale. It is doubtful if in history there has ever been such a massive, wholesale attack on the environment as is occurring in China now.

With money from the World Bank, China has recently carried through several large drainage and desalinization projects along the lower reaches of the Yellow River. I visited one of these less than two years after it was completed. Short-sighted peasants had already filled in many of the tertiary ditches in order to add a few feet to their pitiful small plots. By atomizing landholding and making each family responsible for its own profits and losses the regime has virtually guaranteed such destruction. Neither regulations nor exhortations will stop it. There will never be enough policemen to post one on every ditch.

The Cultural Revolution

The question of blaming Mao for the Great Leap of course leads to that of the Cultural Revolution. Was it a catastrophe, as generally charged? And, if so, must Mao bear sole responsibility? This is a much bigger and more complex question than the one concerning the Great Leap. However, the answer has to focus on much the same problem— the political and social context surrounding Mao's attempt to implement his socialist policy. Here again, one has to deal with the reality of a fundamental split between two headquarters in the Communist Party and the clash between the opposing lines that each was determined to implement.

As things have turned out, it seems clear that Mao correctly appraised the opposition in regard to what it stood for and what it wanted to do with power. Since Mao's death and the dismissal of Hua Guofeng from office, Deng and his group has dismantled, step by step, almost the whole of the economic system and the social and political superstructure built in the first thirty years following liberation, and they are rushing to finish off what remains. The latest proposals for issuing stock indicate that in the future the state hopes to sell off as much as 80 percent of its equity in the whole state sector where, up until now, public ownership has been held up as the guarantee that China still practices socialism. Given the rate at which the regime has escalated the privatization of various sectors in the past, it seems unlikely that the sell off, once begun, will stop at 80 percent or any other percent short of 100. What will be left of socialism then?

Mao foresaw this, called it the "capitalist road," and called Liu and Deng "capitalist roaders." He launched the Cultural Revolution in a major, historically unprecedented campaign to remove them from power and prevent them from carrying out their line. In the end he failed. The important thing to remember at this point is that the Cultural Revolution was indeed a revolution, an enormous class struggle, a form of revolutionary war, if you will, to determine the future of China. It cannot be seen as simply the implementation of some policies by Mao—"'cryptic instructions' while people bowed to his portrait in morning exercises." Just as happened during the Great Leap, but on a much wider scale, the Cultural Revolution unleashed action and counteraction, initiative and counterinitiative, encirclement and counterencirclement, all sorts of excesses, leftist and rightist, and an overall situation that spun out of anyone's control. To blame Mao alone for the disruptions caused by this struggle, for the setbacks and disasters that ensued, is equivalent to the Guomindang blaming the Communists for the disruptions of China's liberation war. "They can't build anything," complained a Guomindang officer to me, "All they can do is blow up bridges and tear up railroad tracks," If there were no Communist-led rebellion, the Guomindang complained, China would be at peace and could get on with reconstruction.

But even though "the tree prefers calm, the wind refuses to sub-side." Class struggle will occur independent of human will. To carry out a program you have to have political power. Those who inherited the wreckage of China's *ancien regime* by virtue of their victory in 1949, inherited also their own class antagonisms, long muted by the threat of a succession of lethal enemies. The struggle between the opposing forces in the form of clashes over land policy broke out even before the last shots of the war died away. Due to historical circumstances peculiar to China, all the politics of the postwar era—all the forces that mattered, all the issues that counted—tended to concentrate inside the Communist Party. Thus the struggle took the form of an internal contest for control of the party and through it for control of the country. Mao saw this phenomenon pretty clearly and began a struggle against the opposition very early. As time went on the struggle escalated, reaching a climax in the Cultural Revolution.

Although Mao won some battles at each stage of the conflict he by no means won the war. He fell far short of accomplishing what he had set out to accomplish when he called on the people to "bombard the headquarters." Instead of consolidating the new ideas, culture, customs, and habits of the working class, which Mao considered vital to the building of socialism, the Cultural Revolution ended in virtual stalemate, with both sides reeling and in society as a whole the three-fold loss of faith described by Deane—loss of faith in the party, in socialism, and in the future; certainly a multiple crisis.

The result was immeasurably complicated by the ultraleft ideology and activity of the gang of four. I do not subscribe to any "gang of five" theory that lumps Mao with his wife and her three cohorts politically, though he certainly was responsible for their coming to prominence to start with. They grossly distorted Mao's policies and directives, carried sound initiatives to extremes that turned them inside out and upside down, and succeeded in wrecking whatever they touched. Although in previous periods Mao had been able to correct both right and "left" excesses, in the 1960s he found himself on "Liang Mountain" in regard to "leftism"—that is, virtually immobilized by a contradiction with the right that he felt tied his hands in dealing with the "left."

There is no question that the Cultural Revolution ended in crisis. The big question is whether the turn to the market was the obvious response for economic sluggishness and whether opening to the world in the indiscriminate way this policy has unfolded was the answer to technological backwardness. It was the obvious response for Deng and associates because that had been their program all along, but was it the best thing for China?

Deane says these policies had been *the alternative* to Maoism since the mid 1950s. But I do not agree. One could argue that China has that alternative today (even though I do not think it is true) but it is very hard to argue that China had that alternative in the 1950s.

In the first place, "opening" was not in China's hands. Mao never chose to cut China off from the West. He was quite willing to establish normal relations with the United States. It was not the Chinese side but the American side that broke all contacts, withdrew its diplomats, ordered its citizens home, and embargoed all trade and all financial exchanges. This embargo was extremely tight, right down to such minor things as the $25 that I wanted to send my daughter in Beijing every month for her support. Under the Trading with the Enemy Act I had to get a Foreign Assets Control license renewed every six months for the transaction. Gene Moy, editor of the *China Daily News,* went to prison in Danbury, Connecticut, for accepting money from the bank of China for an ad concerning the forwarding of remittances from overseas Chinese.

In the second place, China's economy was too weak, at the time, to cope with foreign capital on anything like equal terms. China had a weak banking system, little basic industry, light or heavy, minimal infrastructure—transportation, port facilities, power generating capacity, water supply—a weak commercial network, and a very backward agriculture. Under these circumstances a free market economy combined with an open door, as the door has been thrown open today, would have put the country at the mercy of foreign capital.

In the third place, leaving aside the question of foreign capital, had China relied then on market forces, development would have been extremely one-sided—hot-house growth in certain coastal areas, stagnation for the rest of the country. Central planning allocated investment to every region of the country, building a steel industry in Inner Mongolia, Southeast Shanxi, Sichuan, and Yunnan (to name but a few locations); a chemical industry in Shanxi, Gansu, Hunan, and Heiluongjiang; textiles in Shanxi, Hunan, Hobei, Sichuan; heavy machinery and machine tools in Yunnan, Hunan, Sichuan, Hobei, among others. The *Times Atlas of China*, published in 1974, shows twenty major industrial bases and twenty minor ones scattered across the map of China from north to south, from east to west. Some of them were old (but by then vastly expanded), but most of them were new. Thirty years of hard struggle created the industrial map of modern China after 1949. And in a planned way, taking advantage of natural resources in place and ensuring the development of every region.

In the fourth place, based on the ability of cooperative agriculture to mobilize idle winter labor for capital construction work after 1957, China's peasants greatly improved agricultural infrastructure throughout the country. They terraced millions of acres of hills and mountains, reclaimed riverbank land, vastly expanded the irrigated area, and protected it with windbreaks, thus creating conditions for high, stable yields where none had existed before. Since implementing the contract system, not only has little new capital construction taken place on the land, but the projects and engineering works previously built have not been well maintained. Everywhere the infrastructure, so painstakingly created in the 1960s and 1970s, is falling apart with adverse influence on production.

To say that Deng and associates could have built anything approaching in scale what China built under Mao's leadership with an alternative, mixed economy, free market policy, either on the industrial or on the agricultural front, is sheer speculation. It is one thing to spark a short-lived boom by privatizing collective holdings and giving away to those with an inside track all the public assets created and accumulated over decades. It is quite another to create all this in the first place. It is one thing to enliven the economy by granting easy credit to individual entrepreneurs operating in a sellers market, by granting existing public assets to private managers for commercial-style operation in pursuit of profit, and by attracting foreign investors by making competitive concessions that constantly escalate to the point where they threaten China's autonomy and integrity. It is quite another to build an economy from scratch under fierce foreign embargo to a point where it is strong enough to deal with Western multinational businesses on equal terms and capable of setting parameters for foreign participation that are favorable to China and not simply the first steps toward renewed neocolonial status and eventual debt peonage.

Questionable Policy Claims

This returns us to the point where we began, the question of the current government's claims for the success of the current policies. Deane maintains that peasant incomes have trebled and the gross national product has doubled since the reforms began. Yet with due respect for the State Statistical Bureau's biannual reports, it is certainly advisable, as Deane himself acknowledges, not to suspend disbelief in regard to Chinese statistics.

Certainly one must be skeptical with regard to the trebling of peasant incomes since they abandoned collectives. It is well known that the reform policies were introduced with major price increases for grain that add up over several years to more than 100 percent. So how much of the increased income is due to decreed price rises? This brings up the question of what might have happened to the collective economy if it had remained in place while the price of grain doubled and other prices remained stable. The next question is: Are these income figures corrected for the inflation that came later? One must also ask: Since what constitutes income has to be radically redefined in moving from a collective to a private economy, are Deane's pre and postreform income figures any more comparable than the similar income figures given for Dazhai which I previously analyzed?

When it comes to GNP, the same question arises concerning inflation. And there is a further related issue. Presumably, the GNP includes capital invested in construction. The amounts are surely large. The big question is: How much of the investment is going toward new production and how much toward nonproductive uses primarily housing? All reports indicate that the proportions are way out of balance and that a sharp surge in consumption on top of this investment for consumption is fanning inflation. Any comparison of relative proportions between productive and nonproductive investment before and after the reform would surely favor the former. The charge is, of course, that accumulation rates and investment were too high in the past. That may well be true, but it is also a very serious mistake if these rates are now too low, because then the country is living on printed money, borrowed money, and borrowed time.

Since 1979 there undoubtedly has been a big growth in rural sideline production. To the extent that peasant incomes have risen, they have risen because of price increases for farm products and increased off-the-farm production, not increased farm production. But here also the figures are often distorted, as they have been at Dazhai, in the sense that no credit is given for sidelines that already existed in the past. The whole effort is reported as something that originated with the reform and could not have happened without it, which is a gross distortion. With proper policy from above, sideline production might well have developed faster from a collective base than from a private base.

And the related claim, that the quality of life has improved in China, all depends on how you weigh the various factors. It's a very subjective judgment. Politically, people certainly feel freer, but socially, they are confronting all manner of new and reborn evils—such as prostitution, begging, child-selling, aborted female fetuses, private exploitation, resurgence of disease—everything from syphilis to snail fever—pervasive corruption, and now, worst of all, accelerating inflation. There is a tremendous amount of dissatisfaction, both urban and rural.

Deane writes, "Some systematic undermining is taking place in the countryside as exploitation of labor, access to resources, and political influence create capital assets and economic power. All that is part of the Chinese complexity." True, but the question is, is all that part of building Chinese socialism? Deane's insistence that socialist relations of production remain in contention in the rural areas, is, I think, wishful thinking.

I am quite aware that there are some very successful cooperative villages still functioning in various parts of China, and that they are doing a lot better than their contracting neighbors. They exist because some people had the courage and the opportunity to defy implementation of the responsibility system, to ride out the privatization wind, and to preserve a strong collective core. It would not be too late, if the government decided to rebuild and promote cooperation, for a significant cooperative sector to revive. But so far the government has shown no such inclination. Clearly, no consensus in favor of cooperation has formed at higher levels of the party. Cadres who refused to go along in dissolving coops are still being punished with demotions and transfers. What the planners are now talking about is how best to sell off large chunks of public industry to private or corporate stockholders, not how to reform or rebuild cooperation in the countryside.

In order for coops to revive and grow there must be a suitable climate. Credit policy, price policy, investment policy, mechanization policy, technical policy, inheritance policy, health-care policy, and many others must all favor cooperation. The thrust of culture must encourage "public first, self second" as the ethical norm. Slogans such as "Some must get rich first," "To get rich is glorious," and "Enrich yourself" must be countered. There would have to be a tremendous reversal in the cultural arena—some sort of proletarian counteroffensive that would at least challenge the current monopoly of the whole field by bourgeois standards and ideology.

Finally, Deane says we need the truth about Mao's lamentable practice. The truth we certainly need. But are we getting it from the reformers and their supporters? The basic thesis of these comments is that we are not. If the truth were as Deane outlines, how could one explain the high prestige Mao continues to enjoy so widely in the countryside, on the shop floor, and many other sectors of Chinese life? Successors have been blackening Mao's name for a decade now. Years ago the authorities ordered party committees to remove his portrait from their walls. Last year they sent men with jackhammers to tear down Mao's statue at Beijing University. Mao suddenly disappeared from many other places before and after that incident, though not yet from the Tiananmen Gate. Meanwhile a statue of Liu has been raised up in Beijing.

But in spite of all this, portraits and busts of Mao can be found in millions of peasants', herdsmen's and workers' homes and on many a party committee wall. I have heard so many people say "After all, the old man was right!"

It seems the last chapter has not been written.

大
百 Why Not
阆 the
潮 Capitalist Road?

In the 1930s Chairman Mao declared that the capitalist road was not open to China in the twentieth century. The Chinese revolution against internal feudalism and external imperialism, he said, could not be a democratic revolution of the old type like the British or the French, a revolution to open the road for capitalism, but must be a democratic revolution of a new type, one that would open the road to socialism. In the first place, the imperialist powers would not allow China to carry out any transformation aimed at autonomous capitalist development if they could possibly help it. Every time any section of the Chinese people rose up to challenge traditional rule the powers intervened singly or in unison to suppress the effort by force of arms. This predictable response led Sun Yatsen to ask, "Why don't the teachers ever allow the pupils to learn?" The answer was, of course, that the landlord class as a whole and the compradors in business and government served as the main props of imperialist power in China, hence the latter used all its financial and military might to support, inspire, foster, and preserve these feudal survivals.

Moreover, capitalism was not an option, because as Mao said, "Socialism will not permit it." By this he meant that without allying with and winning support from all the socialist forces in the world—first of all the Soviet Union and second the working classes and working-class movements of Japan, Britain, the United States, France, Germany, Italy, and other countries—and the backing these provided through their own struggles against capitalism and imperialism, the Chinese

164

revolution could not possibly succeed. In the modern era, defined by Mao as an era of wars and revolutions in which capitalism was unquestionably dying and socialism was unquestionably prospering, such an alliance and such support would come only as a response to a Chinese revolution of a new type, a Chinese revolution clearing the ground for working-class power and socialism and not for a Chinese revolution clearing the ground for bourgeois class power and capitalism.

Finally, China's independent national bourgeoisie was weak and vacillating. It could not possibly take on both the Chinese landlords and the imperialists and their Chinese comprador partners without fully mobilizing both the working class and the peasantry. But mobilizing the working class meant putting certain limits on managerial power and meeting certain working-class demands, while mobilizing the peasantry meant carrying out land reform. This could not be done without confiscating the wealth of the landlord class from which the bourgeoisie had, in the main, arisen and to which it still maintained myriad ties. Furthermore, the confiscation of property in land threatened the foundations of all private property and caused the capitalists, much as they desired liberation from feudalism and imperialism, to vacillate. Over and over again the national bourgeoisie proved incapable of firm national leadership against the people's enemies, foreign and domestic. Leading the Chinese democratic revolution thus shifted, by default, to the working class, more numerous by far and older and more experienced than the bourgeoisie, and to the Communist Party that established itself as spokesman for all the oppressed.

New Democracy Proposed

With the Communist Party assuming leadership in the revolution, mobilizing both workers and peasants by the millions, and threatening to confiscate not only all the land of the landlords but all the property of the imperialists and their comprador and bureaucratic allies, the first goal of the revolution could hardly be capitalism. Mao projected a new national form, a mixed economy heavily weighted on the side of public and collective ownership with the joint state-private and wholly private enterprises of the national capitalists playing a minor supporting role. Hence the concept of a New Democratic revolution, a New Democratic transitional period, and a New Democratic state founded after victory with a mandate to carry land reform through to the end and to nationalize the wealth (industrial, commercial, and financial) monopolized by the four ruling families. Once these projects had been completed, the overriding task would be to launch a socialist revolution.

Given the world situation of the 1930s with capitalism in crisis, the Soviet Union booming with new construction, regional wars merging into all-out global war and the third world on the brink of revolution, Mao argued convincingly that China had no choice but socialism. Now fifty years later, at a time when resurgent capitalism demonstrates temporary stability while socialist construction flounders and the "four tigers" of the Pacific Rim (Hong Kong, Taiwan, South Korea, and Singapore) take off, the seers are writing off Mao's compelling logic as anachronistic, irrelevant, even quaint.

In full agreement with the West on the castigation of Mao, China's leaders, after ten years of national and civil war, thirty years of socialist construction, and ten years of capitalist-road reforms, still talk socialism. But they practice massive privatization as they integrate their country as fast as possible into the world market. Optimistic, confident, even arrogant as they were at the start, however, their policy has had enough appalling consequences to place its whole orientation in doubt. And so, like it or not, the old question of whether China can achieve the goal of becoming a strong, modern, independent nation by taking the capitalist road is shouldering its way back onto the agenda.

My view is that autonomous self-generating national capitalism for China is no more viable an option today than it was in 1930, 1950, or 1970. Numerous obstacles stand in the way, some of them extensions of long-standing historical phenomena, others newly created in the course of revolution, land reform and thirty years of socialist construction. Crucial among them are the state of the world economy, the nature of the Chinese state, working-class resistance, and peasant self-sufficiency, the ability of the rural poor to survive on subsistence plots.

In regard to the world economy the strategy of the reformers is to build China into a genuine NIC (newly industrialized country) by following the path pioneered by South Korea, Taiwan, Hong Kong, and Singapore—that is, by taking advantage of the country's cheap labor to solicit foreign capital and start up large-scale manufacture of labor-intensive commodities—primarily textiles but also electric and electronic appliances—for the world market. To this end China created free-trade zones, invested billions in infrastructure, borrowed billions more, and entered the export arena full of hope. But so far China has failed to consolidate an appropriate market share.

This failure has two main causes. First, the expansion of the world market, which once soaked up most offered goods, is now slowing up. As the 1980s wind down, glut not scarcity plagues the globe. The window of opportunity that South Korea and the other "tigers" leaped through is closing fast. Furthermore, they never would have been in a position to make that leap without the economic muscle provided by two protracted American wars for mainland staging grounds against China, wars that called forth decades of heavy American spending on China's open flanks. While many Chinese now look with envy at Taiwan and South Korea and conclude that China took the wrong road, what they fail to understand is that without the challenge which the Chinese revolution posed to the American Century there would be no "tigers" on the Pacific Rim today.

Second, even if the window were still open, even if the market was as lively as ever, it could not hope to absorb the output of a country the size of China. It is one thing for small countries with workforces numbering in single digit millions to tool up for labor intensive exports, but quite another for a Chinese workforce numbering in tens, even hundreds of millions to do the same. It never was reasonable to expect that China could duplicate what small Pacific Rim countries had done. Only a few ever succeeded at it and even those are now moving toward crisis. Other contenders, such as Brazil, Mexico, and India, have run into serious problems without finding any viable road to solvency.

The World Bank strategy of opening third world economies to international market forces by privatizing, liberalizing, making concessions to foreign investors, and concentrating on exports has sharply escalated their dependency on world markets and foreign bank loans. Unable to service their rapidly mounting debts, most of the countries involved have frozen wages, devalued currencies, and cut spending, including spending on vital inputs. Living standards have dropped precipitously. At the same time the cutbacks undermine the economies of the exporting countries, deepening the glut on the supply side of the market. The entire strategy is now clearly bankrupt.

In the final decade of the century the only viable strategy for the third world is to reverse the whole process, diversify, develop internal markets for domestic goods and services and thus reduce dependence. To do this third world countries have to carry out land reform, set up progressive taxation, guarantee workers' rights—all things that China did, was doing, and was doing well prior to the reform. Yet China's leaders still harbor illusions about the NIC model of development, and pin their hopes on a strategy whose time has passed and which for China, given the size of the country and the labor pool available, never could provide an adequate framework for development.

Rice Bowls: Bright, Hard, and Brittle

The internal barriers to capitalist road development in China are today as formidable as the external ones. They can be summed up as (1) the "golden rice bowl"; (2) the "iron rice bowl"; and (3) the "clay rice bowl." The "golden rice bowl" refers to the prerogatives exercised by bureaucrats in office at all levels in the state system over the economy under their control and management and, as a consequence, over their own substantial salaries, fringe benefits, and illicit windfall profits.

The power they wield is essentially feudal, with roots in the highest development of Chinese ancient society, the centralized bureaucratic state where power adhered not to wealth, landed or otherwise, but to government office. Now that, as a consequence of revolution, the government owns most of the economy, official position confers immense and unprecedented economic power. For this reason some young economists have begun to characterize the Chinese system as a "position-power economy." Hua Sheng, Zhang Xuejen, and Luo Xiaoping, writing in the magazine *Economic Research*, used this term recently to describe the present system, one that cannot move toward free market regulation because of government intervention. They bemoan China's failure to establish a functioning national market: "The root cause lies in our failure to separate political power from economic management. The Chinese economy today is, to a significant extent, manipulated by political power. . . . True price reform demands that the country's political as well as economic infrastructure be overhauled." They conclude that "genuinely market oriented reform requires the state to cede its power and responsibility over almost all economic fields to economic bodies. It should allow market participants with full control of their assets to oversee pricing and other economic decisions."[1]

But one may ask: How can these omnipotent bureaucratic powerholders be expected to liquidate their own historical prerogatives and surrender control to technocrats and entrepreneurial upstarts operating under the vagaries of the market? History has no precedent for such behavior. Indeed, this point is argued well in another recent article: "However much the reformer-bureaucrats want to utilize market forces to break through bureaucratic immobilism, they cannot do so," writes Richard Smith, "because to permit real market forces to prevail would destroy the bureaucracy's means of existence and reproduction as a class."[2]

So far the reform in China has ceded some central state power to lower levels such as provinces, major municipalities, and special trading zones, but this has only encouraged lower level bureaucrats to escalate self-enrichment by exercising their local monopoly of power. This often means protecting and advancing regional and sectional interests at the expense of neighbors and the nation. If the reform has dispersed some "position power" it has certainly not dissolved the power system as a whole. Meanwhile, the independent kingdoms where devolved power has come to rest are virtually immune to central control.

How to create a national market in the face of such powerful bureaucratic intervention is a big unresolved problem. No one familiar with Chinese history can be too sanguine about blunting, not to mention abolishing, traditional bureaucratic prerogatives. The whole phenomena poses as big an obstacle to developing socialism as it does to developing capitalism—which is one major reason why Mao launched the Cultural Revolution.

The "iron rice bowl" refers to the guaranteed lifetime jobs and benefits to which all regular workers in state enterprises are entitled. The reformers view these guarantees as the major stumbling block to

1. Hua, Zhang, and Luo, cited in "Top Economists Look Back Over Decade of Reform," *The China Daily*, four-part series, December 1988, pt. 1.
2. Richard Smith, "Class Structure and Economic Reform," paper presented at the Columbia Seminar on Modern China, September 12, 1987, p. 7.

raising labor productivity and modernizing the economy. "Working slowly is fairly common in state-owned factories," write Hua, Zhang, and Luo. "In return for their dependence [on the state] people actually monopolize the work posts they fill. . . . They are guaranteed lifelong tenure and needn't worry about unemployment or bankruptcy."

Reformers long to apply the "stick" of job competition and enterprise failure to these people. They want to transform the relations of production in ways that will force tenured workers onto the labor market and turn their labor power into a commodity—as it must be in any capitalist country.

But from the workers' point of view lifelong job security and its accompanying prerogatives are among the primary accomplishments of the revolution. They are something to cherish and defend. They are what gives meaning to the phrase "the workers are the masters of the factories." If bosses can hire and fire at will, if the reserve army of the unemployed waits to swallow all those rendered redundant for whatever reason, what is left of workers' rights? What is left of socialism?

"Focusing on the lack of free and independent trade unions and the right to strike, [outsiders] assumed that the working class was a helpless controlled victim of the party apparatus," writes James Petras.[3] "A closer view of Chinese factory reality, however, reveals that the Chinese working class operates within a tight network of relations that protect workers from firings, speedup, and arbitrary managerial initiatives, job safeguards that far exceed those found in most Western democracies and would be the envy of many unemployed steel workers." Petras concludes that the reforms are "not only economic reforms but can be more accurately described as socio-political measures designed to restore managerial prerogatives and dismantle the dense network and norms that have been in place since the Revolution."

Viewed realistically, the slowdown on the plant floor is not the inevitable result of the "iron rice bowl," the wonderful job security the revolution has provided for workers, but a response to the "golden rice bowl" of the officials, the managers, the bosses. When cadres take advantage of "position power" to enrich themselves and their offspring "to establish connections to get rare goods, desirable apartments, opportunities for going abroad, promotion and so on,"[4] why should

---

3. James Petras, "Contradictions of Market Socialism in China," unpub. ms., 1987, pp. 5–6.
4. Hua, Zhang, and Luo, *The China Daily.*

wage workers break their backs? In the past those state leaders who were motivated by socialist norms could mobilize the working masses for socialist competition. They could inspire socialist production enthusiasm and achieve "better, faster more economical results." But to do this they had to apply the same set of standards to all. They could not practice self-enrichment up above and expect serve-the-people, build-the-country commitment down below. Unfortunately such officials were far too few in the past and all but nonexistent today.

The reformers, however, do not address the "golden rice bowl" problem. Just the opposite. While paying lip service to socialist morality, they put their faith in making management prerogatives preeminent across the board at the expense of workers' rights and entitlements. They insist on confronting workers with the threat of summary dismissal or job loss due to bankruptcy. They place their faith in fear as the prime source of diligence.

This attitude will inevitably lock the reformers into a showdown battle with a working class that has experienced three decades of socialist relations of production and will not surrender any hard-won right easily. It is a battle that has only just begun, and one which the reformers have no assurance of winning.

Small Plot Security

The "clay rice bowl" refers to the use-rights to the land, which the peasants still retain as the legacy of their land acquisitions during land reform. I call it a clay bowl because the income derived from this source is fragile. Unlike the wages of workers and the salaries of officials, returns from the land depend, in great measure, on sweat, pests, and the weather. Peasants fertilize, till, plant, hoe, and harvest but what they reap will always be, for the most part, beyond their individual control. Their clay rice bowl may reward them bountifully or return nothing at all. Unlike gold or iron it is vulnerable to outside forces and at the mercy of "heaven."

In order to establish capitalism and make the market supreme China's rulers must create conditions for primitive accumulation, which means, first and foremost, separating large masses of peasants from the land and making sure they have nothing to sell but the skills of their hands—in short, turning their labor power into a commodity.

But during the New Democratic revolution in the early 1950s every peasant got a share of that most precious and basic means of production, the land. During the cooperative period they pooled their plots, village by village, to form collectively owned and tilled fields. Decades later the state began to treat collective ownership as public ownership. Thus, when the reform began, what each peasant got was a renewable right to use small plots of publicly owned land for a limited period of years. Quite commonly, during the reform drive, communities first allocated per capita shares, what could be called subsistence plots, to every man, woman, and child, then contracted whatever land remained to those families interested in farming for a living, to those who were willing to raise grain for sale—quota grain for sale to the state at contract prices and surplus grain for sale to the market at whatever price it might bring. Under this system a substantial proportion of the cropland in China lies outside the sphere of commerce. It provides a food source of last resort to the rural masses regardless of conditions in the general economy. The underemployed and ill-equipped peasants, given good weather, can probably survive on these miniscule holdings. To prosper, however, the ablebodied laborers among them must set up nonfarm sidelines or seek work beyond the village. Either way, they tend to neglect the land, farming it indifferently, even letting it lie idle when wage work expands, transport booms, and peddling pays, then skimming off whatever crop they can coax from the neglected soil when the downturn comes.

The reformers hoped and planned that after the break-up farming specialists would be able to contract use-rights from less committed neighbors and create holdings of scale suitable for mechanization and scientific management. But since most small holders regard their plots as social insurance against unemployment, enterprise failure, or other personal disaster such as illness or old age, few have been ready to yield up their per capita use-rights to others even when they do not exercise them themselves. What this means overall for Chinese agriculture is that a substantial part of the nation's scarce cropland, all of which ought to produce to the utmost, will produce at far below its potential for a long time to come.

Recent developments—the sudden withholding of credit, the shutting down of thousands of construction sites, the failure of thousands of small rural enterprises—threw millions of peasants out of off-farm work. This demonstrated as nothing else could that peasant reluctance to part with per capita land-use rights was shrewdly grounded. But this same reluctance also means that the conditions for primitive accumulation in China cannot easily be satisfied. The reforms cannot easily reduce peasant labor power to a commodity in the usual sense, nor can they easily make all land marketable. Per capita land use rights as distinct from contracted rights, though theoretically subject to lease or purchase, are not often surrendered. In the long run food production suffers serious erosion. Those who control the use-rights, the peasant masses, cannot and do not utilize them to the full, while those who might develop their potential, the crop-raising specialists, cannot get their hands on them.

Crop specialists, on their part, contracting only the land that is left after the per capita distributions, also work only scattered strips of land, the pathetic "noodle strips" that now characterize Chinese farmland; hence their labor productivity is extremely low. Few can make as much money by farming as they can by leaving the land. Consequently, to keep people farming community after community has to subsidize the contractors with free materials and services.

Privatization has thus created a situation that all but guarantees agricultural stagnation. Without a sound agricultural base there is little chance for the rest of the economy to prosper. Beijing authorities are blaming this year's chronic power shortages on lack of coal, which in turn they blame on lack of transport, which in turn they blame on lack of power. But if one looks more deeply into the problem one finds that Shanxi coal has been in short supply all winter because the itinerant miners who staff the private and the collective mines responsible for half the province's production have quit in droves because they could not afford grain at this years inflated free market prices. So the power shortage really stems from the grain shortage. All the above phenomena—the glut on the commodity markets of the world, especially in labor-intensive industrial goods, the "golden rice bowl," the "iron rice bowl," and the "clay rice bowl"—none of which are easy to exorcise—make the capitalist road a very arduous and uncertain one for China to take.

Even if China could somehow overcome the barriers en route, it would still only achieve, as Petras has pointed out, an economy plagued as other third world economies have been by "short-term growth punctured by long-term stagnation; foreign dependence, leading to capital inflow in boom periods and outflow during crises; and management controls that maximize competitiveness but provoke adversarial class relations."[5] These are hardly consequences that favor the creation of an autonomous self-generating economy capable of providing a reasonable level of prosperity for a majority of the Chinese people.

---

5. Petras, "Contradictions," p. 1

大回潮 Tiananmen Massacre: June 1989

It's impossible to describe everything that happened recently in China. I'd like to concentrate on the two crucial days that marked the watershed, June 3 and 4, June 3 being the last day of triumphant demonstrations, and June 4 being the massacre by part of the army. On June 3 I was fortunate in being able to spend the whole day in the square, and it was no longer massed with students. There were only scattered student groups in the square on June 3, most of them from outside of Beijing. Large numbers of Beijing students had already left, not to go back to their campuses, but to go out into the community and factories to organize. They were still very active in trying to promote a large people's movement. The students from the very beginning—I'm not sure from what dates—had set up a broadcasting unit—well, it's really a loudspeaker—in one corner of the square, and on the morning of June 3 there was a journalist talking on the loudspeaker describing the events of the night before, some of which were quite bizarre.

First, a group of soldiers dressed in shorts and T-shirts came running down Changan Avenue trying to get into the square, posing as civilians. They didn't carry any weapons, of course, but they did not get very far down the avenue before they were blocked and turned back. Out on the west side of the city a little van skidded and went over a barrier and hit four people on bicycles, one of whom died, and then the people held this van while the three cars that were with it made their

---

This is a slightly revised version of a talk given at the CUNY Graduate Center, New York City, July 13, 1989.

175

escape. And they found inside the van soldiers in plain clothes with weapons and steel cables for tying around people's necks, to hook them up to each other. In other words, it was a secret army mission that was inadvertently exposed because the driver skidded and had an accident. This was the big news of June 3.

The whole city was alert to any move by the military or by the police. I don't really have a count of how many hundreds of thousands of people were involved, but I'm sure that overall, from the two weeks following the declaration of martial law, until June 3 or 4, certainly several million citizens of Beijing became active. But somehow that didn't come through in the media, I think, because the journalists were all concentrating on the square. Almost all the networks had their camera teams in the square, and the focus of world publicity was on Tiananmen Square.

But the big events were happening on the outskirts of the city, in layers more or less corresponding to the ring roads around the city where the people were blocking the armies from coming in. Every night, all night long, thousands of people blocked just about every intersection. I happened to live in the northeast corner of the city near what they call the third ring road, which wasn't a major entry point. But every night people gathered there, one to two thousand of them. They went to the bus parking lot and pushed buses by hand across the intersection, blocking it all four ways. Then, since there were still gaps, they stopped coal trucks, and freight trucks, and got them to fill in the gaps. There was also a brigade of motorcycle riders supporting the students. They came out at night, some 300 strong, and cruised around the city, full of enthusiasm. I remember one night when they came by. There was just enough of a gap for them to get through and everyone gathered to watch them. Then one of the trucks that had been persuaded to stop decided that he would take off. No one got very upset. They just stopped the next vehicle that came down, a farmer with a two-wheel tractor with a little trailer behind, and on the trailer a huge fishing boat, and in the fishing boat was the man's whole family. They persuaded him to block the gap, so the peasant and his family in the fishing boat spent the night there. I hate to think what might have happened to that family had the army come that night!

On June 3 in the square students broadcast all the news of the night before and then a young professor got up and announced the formation of a People's University which was to be held in the square starting that night. That was probably one of the more short-lived universities in the world. I believe, in fact, it did get underway, but not for long. If one could have stood there all day and listened it would have been fascinating, just to hear what came across that loudspeaker. But then rumors circulated that there were actually soldiers on the west side of the Great Hall. That was the first time soldiers had been reported as being that close to the square. We went over to investigate. And sure enough, there's sort of a pit to the west side of the north steps of the Great Hall of the People, and down in this recessed area there were 200 soldiers. Some of the people were cursing them, and some trying to mobilize them. But the soldiers had orders not to fraternize, so they were sitting facing inward, very shame-faced, and trying to ignore what people were saying all around them. We went close enough to see these soldiers, and all of a sudden—it was about two o'clock in the afternoon—8,000 troops poured out of the Great Hall. It was an enormous cascade of helmeted troops, without visible weapons, but each of them carrying a little satchel—presumably they either had hand grenades or tear gas grenades or weapons in these satchels. So they came out apparently determined to get into the square. As they poured out in three streams, they formed ranks of eight, then started rushing northward up the street. People appeared, it seemed from nowhere, and in a few seconds they jammed the whole north end of the street. Some young people ran toward the soldiers and threw themselves against their chests! Some of them bounced off and fell down, and the soldiers kept running forward, but the people kept running south, and finally, even though the ranks behind were pushing the ranks ahead the soldiers couldn't move forward any more. And then, since there were 8,000 troops those in back just folded up like an accordion against the front end. The officers ordered them to move to the left, and they'd all move across the street to the left, and then there would be a new order—"No, no, not so far, get back to the middle." There was this huge dragon of troops writhing back and forth in the street. We thought it might get fairly ugly, so we started west down a small roadway that ran parallel to Chang An. We got to the next intersection just as hundreds of people came screaming down the street yelling "Tear gas! Tear gas!" Some armed police had used tear gas in front of the Central Committee headquarters, Zhongnanhai, so we decided that wasn't the best way to leave. We had bicycles, so we turned back and found a little alley that ran south, and we came out at the Colonel's Kentucky Fried Chicken restaurant.

The contrast of trying to get away from 8000 troops and nearly being tear-gassed and then coming to the Colonel's air-conditioned, three-story building, girls in short skirts and little chicken hats, and the choice of two pieces or five pieces of tender chicken, and ice-cold Coke, was enough to blow your mind away! So, being hungry and thirsty we went up to the second floor and tried to catch a glimpse of what might be happening in the square, but couldn't see anything.

Loudspeakers Silenced

We finally left there and went back to the square. By that time the government had figured out a way to hook up the speakers that are in front of Tiananmen and they started blaring a condemnation of the democracy statue that the students had put up. Many people think it was a copy of the Statue of Liberty—of course, it did get some inspiration from the Statue of Liberty, but it was a very Chinese statue, nevertheless. The girl looked most like Liu Hulan a hero of the anti-Japanese war, no crown of spikes on her head, and she was holding the torch with both hands. It was not simply a copy of the Statue of Liberty, as the American press tried to make out. It expressed much of what the students felt in terms of democracy. The voice on the loudspeakers began to attack this thing as an alien intrusion and a mockery of Chinese culture. As we watched, some students climbed up the poles one by one and cut the wires to the loudspeakers, and it must have been 220 current because they were getting heavy shocks from the pliers as they cut, and they asked for cloth and gloves to protect their hands. Huge crowds blocked the whole area right across Chang An Street, watching as the students cut one wire after the other. There were ten speakers altogether. After the pliers silenced them you could hear the students' own speaker once again. It was a rather triumphant process.

Later we went back to see what was happening with the troops, still bottled up behind the Great Hall. We parked our bikes under the wall of the Forbidden City. The wall brandished chalked slogans that were quite provocative. One was a mock conversation between Deng Xiao-ping and Li Peng and went something like "Uncle Deng, what do we do now?" And Deng Xiaoping says, "Well, I'm not sure. We'll have to wait and see, but I think the best thing is for me to sacrifice you to save me." A little further down there was another slogan in chalk that was, in hindsight, prophetic. It said, "Better listen to Deng. He has the guns." We went back and found most of the troops sitting in the street absolutely exhausted, and the students of the medical college were trying to make life more comfortable for them. They were filling their canteens with water, bringing them food, trying to fraternize, and the crowds were singing revolutionary songs. Every time they'd finish a song they'd say *Jie feingjun, lai yi ge* ("Army, you sing one!"), and finally as the sun was setting a soldier stood up and tried to lead a response, and just then the officers ordered the whole bunch of troops back into the hall. Whether they were trying to prevent that fraterniza-tion or whether the order had just come down, I don't know. But the soldiers went back into the hall single file; it took them more than an hour to get back, running. Everyone was standing around cheering, feeling that the people had won a great victory. There was one student who was standing near us—we were only about two feet from where the soldiers were running in—and he was cautioning the crowd. He said, "Don't feel too happy. This is only 8,000 men. There are 300,000 more out there and they can take the square at any time . So the worst is yet to come." I thought he was being pessimistic, but of course his words turned out to be quite accurate.

Gunfire at Night

We finally left the square abut nine o'clock, and being ice cream addicts, we stopped at the Jianguo Hotel to have some ice cream on the way home. I think one of the guards there didn't like where I put my bicycle: he let the air out of my bicycle tire, and at ten o'clock or so we started home with a flat tire on the bike. Things seemed a little ominous. A huge crowd of people blocked an army truck at the over-pass just beyond. We decided not to worry about a flat tire, and went all the way home on the rim. We got home about 10:30 and fell asleep exhausted. Already at that hour the shooting had started on the western side of the city. The first casualties occurred when some troops of the 27th Army fired on some people in front of the Military Museum of the Revolution at the western end of Chang An Street. But we didn't know that was happening and slept peacefully. We were awakened about two in the morning by very heavy fire on the eastern side of the city, not just automatic weapons fire, but big guns, like guns on tanks. The army personnel carriers had big guns but nothing that could be called artillery. We heard heavy firing as the army came in from the east as well as the west. If the "Nightline" program I saw is typical of the television coverage, that showed personnel carriers on fire arriving in the square and being attacked by people, which gives a completely wrong impression of the sequence of events. It looked as though the people were on the offensive and the army was on the defensive. Actually, by the time these vehicles got to the square, they had shot their way through barricade after barricade and had killed probably close to 2,000 people. Arriving in the square was the end of the assault, not the beginning of it. Once the army began to shoot down people, they got very angry and became active and counterattacked in any way they could. The Chinese television programs followed the same pattern; they showed the end first. They took scenes from Sunday afternoon where the people were burning tanks and weapons carriers and put them at the beginning. They said, "This is Saturday afternoon and this is the way people treated our poor soldiers. So our soldiers had no choice but to hit back." Actually they reversed the days, and made out that the soldiers were the victims of the people, which was just a complete lie. The army came in shooting and they killed people all the way down the avenue. And they kept killing people even after they secured the square.

Now, it's true that the soldiers didn't kill all the students in the square. There was, in fact, not really a massacre in the square. There were about 4,500 students left, and they gathered around the Martyrs Monument and negotiated with the soldiers about being allowed to leave, which was agreed, and the bulk of them did leave. Some of them after they left got run down by a tank. I think it killed eleven, running them down from behind, but there are persistent rumors that a hundred or more refused to leave and they were shot in the square. Personal friends of mine were in the Beijing Hotel all night. They said there was heavy firing in the square about four o'clock in the morning at a time when all the lights went out. There are so many different versions that it's very hard to prove. One of the problems is that most of the media left the square with the main body of the students, so there were no reporters around when the remnant group apparently defied the army and were killed.

But regardless of what happened in the square, the main killing occurred on Chang An Street both in the east and the west. On Sunday morning we went to see my sister and brother-in-law, who live out north of the city in Changping county. Since my brother-in-law had just had a serious operation we hired a little minibus to take us there. The driver had been up all night roaming the eastern end of Chang An Street and described the scenes he saw. He said the army came in shooting and behind them were army ambulances picking up the bodies and taking them away in order to conceal the casualties. He thought at least a thousand had been killed by the eastern attack, not to mention what happened at the other side of the city. Of course, all of those figures are guesses, presumably exaggerations because when you have a slaughter like that it's so gruesome and so upsetting that it's easy to make figures bigger than they are. However, he was very angry and upset and as we went north we came across army vehicles burning and every time he saw one he was so happy.

We went out to the countryside, spent part of the day there and came back into the city about five o'clock. We passed a whole convoy of trucks burning north of a place called Desheng Gate. Eighteen trucks and command cars were burning, with flames forty or fifty feet in the air, fuel tanks exploding, and tires melting. It was a fantastic sight. Apparently the soldiers had been blocked from driving and had walked on into the city. Then the people burned the entire convoy. Later, another convoy stopped there. By Monday afternoon there were thirty-three burned-out vehicles outside Desheng Gate.

Death in the Afternoon

At five o'clock when I got back into the city I had a chance to go down to the Beijing Hotel, where a close friend of mine had a room on a high floor and I went up there to see what was still going on at the square. The square was completely secure; there were two rows of soldiers blocking Chang An Street, and behind them a row of tanks, and behind those a whole rectangle of personnel carriers. The people kept coming from the east and getting as close as they dared to the troops and shouting at them, most of them trying to persuade them to cease and desist from killing people. Whenever 200–250 people gathered there the soldiers fired point blank and mowed them down. I only witnessed the last time this happened, but my friends who had been there all day and kept notes said it happened at least six times. Just about every hour on the hour it was time to shoot down the people, and they counted fifty bodies carried out of there assumed dead, not to mention the wounded. The army wouldn't allow any ambulances to go in, so the people who brought the bodies out were these pedicab men, some of whom have little freight bikes. They would rush in even while the firing was going on and pick up the casualties. At the time I saw this happen, the firing was absolutely intense and it lasted five minutes. How anyone survived it, I don't know. The only warning the victims had was that when the soldiers were about to fire, they ran forward a few steps, then aimed and fired. So during that second when they ran forward, people could drop to the ground. But each time, of course, people were killed, people were wounded, and some who ran away were shot in the back. It was a most gruesome sight. The killing was absolutely unnecessary because the whole of Chang An Street was under control . The army had cleaned out the square and there was no reason to think that 200 people, most of whom had come only to talk could in fact threaten armed men. The response from the people that last time was to set fire to the last bus that still sat unburned in front of the Beijing Hotel. Flames and smoke billowed out and blew down in the soldiers' faces and obscured the people who were shot, so it was hard at that time to tell how many were killed or wounded.

I left the hotel about 10:30 that night and went back up Wangfujing toward the Palace Hotel to try to find a taxi or some way to get home. A young man came out of the Peking Union Medical College (PUMC) Hospital with his lacerated hands all bandaged. He asked if I could help him get home. He lived beyond where I lived, and he said that he had been shot at the time when I was watching and that his bicycle had been completely destroyed. We were able to find a pedicab and I took him home. On the way, of course, we had time for a long conversation and I asked him why on earth he went up there. Didn't he know that they were still shooting people? He said he had to go and tell them not to shoot. He told them that we're the people and you're the People's Army and you shouldn't be killing people. He said he thought they would fire in the air, but instead they fired parallel to the street. He dropped to the ground but a bullet hit the pavement, broke up and lacerated his hands. He was lucky that's all that happened to him.

Later, when we checked at a nearby hospital we found that the bullets used were a type of explosive bullets. They leave a very small entry wound but do very large damage inside. They seemed to be hollow bullets or spiral bullets or some kind of dumdum bullets that made terrible wounds causing heavy internal bleeding. Many wounds that wouldn't ordinarily be serious became very serious. People were afraid to stay in the hospital. They thought the troops might come and arrest them, so they got a little first aid and then went home. So many people died at home. By Wednesday of that first week there were close to a hundred unclaimed bodies in the PUMC hospital and sixty-seven unclaimed bodies in the Fuxing Hospital and similar high numbers in other hospitals around. So just the number of unclaimed bodies in the morgues of the hospitals outnumbered the total number of people the government claimed had been killed, and of course those numbers include only the ones who died in the hospital after coming for treatment. Many people were killed on the street and other people went through the hospital and died at home. So certainly the casualties were as high as 2,000, while many, many thousands more were wounded. It was a major, major assault on the people.

Teach the People a Lesson

I think the purpose of the assault didn't have so much to do with the students. It was pretty clear that if the government had waited another week or so there would have been almost no students in the square. They had done just about all they could do to raise issues and organize and mobilize. They had welcomed colleagues from all over the country, but more people were leaving every day than were arriving and the numbers were dwindling. If the authorities had waited another week, probably the square would have been quiet, and if the square had been quiet, the people would not have been mobilizing at night to prevent the army from coming to clear the square. There would have been no need for a military assault. But I think that Deng was extremely upset by the mobilization of people, by the millions that went into action. He was frightened by them, and he set out to punish them. You know, Deng is a man who likes to teach people a lesson. He sent the army into Vietnam to teach the Vietnamese a lesson, and of course, the Vietnamese taught the Chinese army a lesson. It wasn't necessary to use military force, but he wanted to send a strong signal to the people of China concerning who was boss, so he moved with force.

You may question why he didn't move sooner. Why didn't he move at the time martial law was declared? Well, the fact is that at that time, about May 20 or 21, the army that was available around Beijing, the 38th, refused to shoot, refused to take the people on. When the soldiers tried to come into the city, they were blocked by the barricades and the mass of people, and rather than kill people to force their way into the city, they either just sat there or retreated. After that Deng removed the commanders of the 38th army from office and courtmartialed them but he still had to find other troops and it took him about two weeks going around the country to find the troops who would shoot, and then he had to move them in. The troops that would shoot turned out to be the 27th army, which was the army President Yang Shangkun personally commanded in the past. It is now commanded by his nephew. This army is made up of Sichuan troops. Everyone in Beijing said they came from Shenyang, other accounts said Shijiazhuang or inner Mongolia, but in Beijing they thought they came from Shenyang, which is in the Northeast. Nevertheless they were Sichuan troops. Yang Shangkun is a Sichuan man, Deng Xiaoping is a Sichuan man, Li Peng is a Sichuan man. In China, you know, they call Sichuan people Sichuan rats, so there are three rats in charge of China at this point. But the fact is that that army was willing to shoot. It seems they did take part in the invasion of Vietnam ten years ago and they killed civilians there. People said they were about ten years older than the average recruit in the 38th army, 40th army, and other participating units. For whatever reason, they were not reluctant to fire and of course they had been isolated from the news before they moved. They had been told that people had been killing soldiers and mistreating them, so they were mobilized to defend themselves and to defend the army. In any case, they did come in shooting. I was not surprised that Deng would order armies to shoot, but I was surprised that he found armies that were willing to do so under those circumstances. So the delay was to find the right troops.

In the days that followed the massacre the government spent enormous energy trying to track down and punish both the student leaders involved and the leading people involved in resisting the army. They seized at random people they accused of having burned trucks or, in the case of Shanghai, having burned a train. They tried them, condemned them to death, gave them three days to appeal, and then shot them, as you know. They also issued warrants for twenty-one student leaders and arrested six or seven of them. Others, as you know, got away. The leaders of the nation paid extraordinary attention to taking revenge on the people and on the activists and of course they condemned the whole thing as a "counterrevolutionary insurrection."

Speaking Truth to Power

One of the heroes on the people's side at this time was Yang Xianyi. He is known to many people in the West as the editor of the Panda series of Chinese translations "The Dream of the Red Chamber," other classics, and current Chinese literature. Xianyi and Gladys Yang have been doing this work for many years. On Sunday night, the fourth of June, BBC television interviewed him and he condemned the action as a fascist coup, probably the worst atrocity in modern Chinese history. He took a very strong stand. He expected that he would be arrested forthwith, and the next day his family persuaded him to hide away. He hid out for a few days and then decided that was hardly worth doing. So he reappeared. Just a few days before I came home I went to see him and we had a long talk. He agreed with me. "You know," he said, "I'm a Communist." It seems he joined the Communist Party not so long ago at a time when they were trying to mobilize prominent intellectuals to join, since the reforms began ten years ago. He said, "I'm not going to resign from the party. I think they've besmirched the name of the party, they've dragged the army through the mud, and we're going to stand up and fight." Of course, he's absolutely defenseless there, yet he's taken such a strong stand . . .

When I went to leave, my bicycle was out on the street. He saw me out to my bike, and in front of the market and hundreds of people, most of whom knew who he was, gave me a big hug, and sent me on my way. He's, I think, about seventy-four years old, an old man—I'm only seventy—and I had the sense that he was prepared for whatever might happen, that he felt that this was the time to stand up and be counted, that he didn't really care what might befall him. As far as I know, and strange to say, they made no move against him, and of course that's probably pretty smart on the part of the government, and yet they were doing so many irrational things it wasn't all that clear whether they would act wisely or not in this case. If there's any single Chinese intellectual who is well known in the West and particularly in England—he graduated from Oxford—it's Yang Xianyi.

His stand inspired me, to a certain extent, to take a similar position, and to speak out as widely and as forcefully as possible, and to publicly state that I would not do any further work for this government, not until the government in China reverses the verdict on the student movement. Until they are ready to say that it is a patriotic revolutionary movement and not a counterrevolutionary insurrection, I will not do any more work for agricultural construction. My job there was to help set in motion a project which I've been trying to convince the government to do for ten years. It involved setting up model villages in different crop areas of China that would then use the best modern machinery possible. After ten years of effort we finally got it off the ground. It's being financed by the United Nations and the United Nations Food and Agriculture Organization, and should commence in November. It will last for three years with a two-year extension, a five-year project. I will not have anything more to do with it until and when the verdict is reversed.

A Squandered Mandate

You may ask what I think the future holds in that respect. I think this government is very shaky, that Deng Xiaoping has really lost his mandate. Deng and his colleagues have alienated a large part of the army, alienated a large part of the party, and the vast majority of the Chinese people—they have really no leg to stand on. They're ruling only with the gun and with terror. The only thing that's holding the government together is Deng Xiaoping, his very fast political footwork, playing off one commander against another, one leader against another, and summoning all those old octogenarians back. Many people think of them as being hardliners, who somehow believe in socialism. I think if you examine the list of those people that he has been able to mobilize, almost every one of them was named by Mao Zedong as a capitalist roader. They are not a group of men who have stood for socialism in the last ten years—quite the contrary. Although they may not have been as active as Zhao and Hu Yaobang in breaking up socialism, they certainly haven't stood in the way.

There are differences among the people in this ruling group, but the differences relate to the pace and scale of privatization, to the mix of planning and free market, and so on. They are certainly not trying to build socialism—they're *all* capitalist roaders. And they've developed beyond that to the point of being bureaucratic capitalists with strong comprador tendencies. The one thing that united China in this movement was the disgust at corruption. The level of corruption in China has reached proportions similar to the those that overwhelmed the Guomindang back before 1949. What made it possible was, on one hand, the development of a free market, and on the other, state-controlled prices and quotas and a big state intervention. People with clout, people in high office, have been able to use their influence to buy commodities at low prices from the state and turn around and sell them at high prices on the free market. In this way they have been able to make huge fortunes which everyone in China believes are being salted away in Swiss bank accounts, in real estate deals, and so on. I think that this is certainly true. And the people who are doing this are mainly the sons and daughters of the top people. Zhao's sons are deeply involved, Deng Xiaoping's sons are deeply involved, though apparently Li Peng's sons are not. Yang Shangkun's whole family is involved and they're deeply involved in the whole army as well.

So you have what could be called the development of bureaucratic capitalism, government officials who are taking over huge chunks of industry and combining them as private fortunes and then making comprador deals with external capitalists. It's one of the ironies of the whole situation in Beijing—that the big new hotels are joint ventures. The Beijing Hotel, wholly owned by China, was virtually abandoned.

After the massacre you couldn't get any food there, the lights weren't even on in the lobby. There was a bullet hole in the glass above the front door. The press kept rooms there because from the upper balconies you could see what was happening in the square, but once the army consolidated its position in the square, once it stopped shooting people, then having a room there wasn't that advantageous. Furthermore, there were always rumors that the army was going to sweep everybody out, so the Beijing Hotel virtually shut down and everyone moved to the Palace Hotel. Now that's a different story. It's the newest, most luxurious hotel in the city. It has a two-story waterfall in the lobby that continuously tumbles down into the open basement and a Watson's supermarket underground. Strange to say, it's owned by the army in conjunction with a group of Manila capitalists—talk about comprador arrangements. And the beautiful waitresses there look Chinese but they don't speak Chinese. They speak Tagalog and English but not Chinese. It's strange for someone like me to try to communicate with them in Chinese. They look back at me with completely blank stares. Well, the Kunlun Hotel is another new hotel—this one done in Texas modern style with stainless steel pillars and all that stuff. It's jointly run by the security forces and different outside capitalists.

Of course, many of you know that I have been a critic of the reforms in China since they began, starting with the dissolution of cooperative agriculture. The surprising thing to me is the speed with which these reforms brought China to the crisis it's in today. The crisis is the direct outcome of reform policies, of the privatization of agriculture, the attempted privatization of industry, of the free market and of the decentralization which threw important economic decisions to regions, particularly coastal regions who then, making money fast and loose, bid against interior China for scarce goods, particularly raw materials. Conditions developed that brought the country close to economic chaos. The government could not guarantee supplies, power was cut down so much that factories worked two or three days instead of six, prices soared out of control, corruption became endemic, and all the moral degradation of the old society started to come back.

You have open prostitution, you have begging (you actually have the return of child mutilation so children can beg better), you have a huge pool of unemployed—last winter there were 50 million people uprooted from the countryside, who had no employment in the cities. In order to combat inflation the government shut down 10,000 construction projects and created 4 or 5 million more unemployed. You have these enormous contradictions all arising directly out of the reform. You have the virtual collapse of the birth control, family planning program. The birth rate is now much higher than China has acknowledged. You have a crisis in education particularly in rural areas but also in the cities where funds are so short that they can't pay teachers adequately. They say if your money isn't enough, you should moonlight on another job. You have this weird situation where teachers in the classroom are running ice cream concessions and soda pop stands, and trying to find second jobs and third jobs and of course neglecting their teaching. And then of course you have the privatization of health care particularly at the grassroots level. There is an across-the-board decay of normal services and normal service standards, so that everyone is becoming angry.

The peasants have figured Deng out quite well. They have the impression that every time a problem arises, Deng will make a snap decision as to what to do about it and then, of course, the results often turn out less ideal than they should. Then he makes another snap decision which turns out even worse than the preceding one—a whole series of pragmatic decisions. So the peasants say "You no sooner think of it than you say it, you no sooner say it than you do it, you no sooner do it than it's a mess." And so it seems to be in one area after another. I believe that this massacre of the people of Beijing is exactly one of those terrible mistakes which Deng has made. In an effort to solve one problem he has jumped into much, much worse problems.

Of course, the Western media is presenting this as the last gasp of Communism and the ultimate result of having carried out a revolution, but it is not that at all. It's the ultimate result of having betrayed the revolution ten years ago. I haven't had the time to go back and search out those very cogent statements that Chairman Mao made about Deng, Liu, Shaochi, and other capitalist roaders. On many separate occasions he said that if these people come to power our party will change color and we will end up with a fascist regime, and then the Chinese people will rise up and will again conduct revolution and change this. The only surprising thing to me is how fast this happened. Ten years ago Deng was a very popular man. Ten years ago he was supposedly saving China from the debacle of the Cultural Revolution and putting China back on its feet by introducing a measure of freedom and discussion, a free market and other liberating innovations. And here, ten years later, there is absolute military dictatorship, everyone is being forced to agree that a counterrevolutionary insurrection broke out that the army did exactly the right thing and that the organizers of this movement should be persecuted and punished.

One of the last things that happened to me in Beijing before I came home was that an old friend who is a party member came to me and said, "Yesterday we had our party meeting and we all had to *biaotai* (that is express an attitude) and we had to say the army had acted justly in suppressing a counterrevolutionary insurrection. I also said those words, and I was lying and I've been lying so often, so many times and I'm sick of it, but I have to live here, I have to support my family. I have to lie in this circumstance, but I'm only hoping that you will be able to go home and not lie about what happened here."

A Hugh Progressive Coalition

The truth is, the students were not conducting an insurrection at all. They were not trying to overthrow the government. They were demanding Deng's resignation because he is eighty-four years old, corrupt, and his policies are jeopardizing China's future. And they are demanding the resignation of Li Peng primarily because he imposed martial law. Prior to the martial law decree they were asking for dialogue, a freer press, more democratic rights, public disclosure of high officials' assets. This is not equivalent to demanding the overthrow of the government; nor is calling on certain leaders to resign insurrectionary. This happens frequently in other countries, most recently in Japan, twice. But Deng regarded it as a terrible affront, as turmoil, as chaos, and he punished them for it.

Many people on the left in this country worry about the politics of the students: Aren't they rightists? Aren't they making bourgeois demands? Aren't they attacking socialism? Well, there is a lot of political diversity among the students; many of them look to Western capitalism as a model. They have rediscovered Adam Smith and the market and they harbor serious illusions about both. But the students are not the right wing in Chinese politics. The right wing consists of Deng and his group. The students are part of a huge progressive coalition—people in the middle, people to the left of the middle, and even some to the right of the middle—that is attacking the real reactionaries. Furthermore, as the movement develops it has to move to the left, and it is moving to the left. The students, on their own, do not have the power to transform China. To do that they have to go to the people, and when they go to the people they have to start dealing with the nitty-gritty issues of peasants' rights and workers' rights. They have to defend land-use rights and protect peasants against adverse price scissors. They have to stand with the workers against surrendering all prerogatives to management. They have to defend the "iron rice bowl," the job security workers won through revolution.

Some people in the United States are calling for the establishment of a new revolutionary party in China and the launching of a new revolution. My estimate is that there are large numbers of dedicated communists in the Chinese Communist Party and also in the army. I foresee the possibility of change brought about by the mobilization of such people—perhaps through an army coup led by radical officers who can rally all the revolutionary elements in the army, in the party, and in society.

In sum, I think there is a lot of naiveté among the students and their supporters, but I also think they lost some of it on June 3 and 4.